I0500069

Money, Speculation, and Fraud. |

A History of Financial Speculation and Fraud

Anddy Park

About the Author

Anddy Park

Andy is the Finance Director of Yuil Technology Investment, a South Korean venture capital firm, and is a core manager of its venture capital fund.

He has worked as a venture capitalist at KDB Capital and as an auditor at Choeun Savings Bank. He has also served as CEO of Yuil Capital Partners and CareerNet, and has a wide range of experience from business consulting to venture capital to consumer finance.

During his more than 10 years as a financial institution executive, he has seen how changes in the macroeconomic environment can determine the fate of financial institutions.

He has been thinking a lot about how to survive an economic crisis, and he began to be interested in the causes and consequences of economic crises, especially when he observed the restructuring of financial institutions and companies in 1997 and 1998, when Korea applied for an IMF bailout. This book is the result of his interest.

He majored in economics at Korea University in Seoul, South Korea, and is the author of The ABCs of financial technology.

MONEY, SPECULATION, AND FRAUD. I

A HISTORY OF FINANCIAL SPECULATION AND FRAUD

ANDDY PARK

Contents

Prologue

It is said that history is a mirror of the future. This is because we can find similar cases in the past, analyze them, and get hints on how to solve problems or find solutions to problems that are happening now or are expected to happen in the future.

History is full of stories about the intrinsic properties of money, the desires of those who handle it, and the psychology of greed.

These events and the stories of speculators, investors, and fraudsters provide a wealth of inspiration that can be applied to modern-day phenomena involving various forms of finance and investment.

From the Dutch tulip mania of the 17th century to Ponzi schemes and other forms of investment fraud, speculation and financial fraud that capitalize on human greed have consistently threatened all economic actors.

Especially in the 18th century, when France and Britain were experiencing severe financial crises due to the financial strains of war, the various proposals they considered to solve their debt crises have provided many ideas for today.

The Mississippi Company and South Sea Company bubble bursts, in which the state exchanged state debt for private equity, were essentially similar to the leveraged buyouts that are common in turnarounds of distressed companies today.

The idea of solving the government's debt problem by exchanging privately held government bonds for shares of state-owned enterprises (SOEs), which boosted the stock price of the SOEs, and in the process solved the problem of circulation of government-issued money, which was not trusted as money, has had a profound impact on human economic history.

The idea of solving the government's debt problem and the circulation of money by harnessing investors' speculation in an era when capitalism was not fully established is remarkable. However, it is an unfortunate side effect that the methods they used to prop up stock prices have been inherited by similar stock manipulation schemes today, which are creating more victims.

Throughout history, there have been many examples of countries that have run up huge fiscal debts due to a variety of spending factors, and many people have come up with creative ideas to solve these fiscal crises.

Let's say the U.S. government, which is facing a huge national debt due to its massive issuance of government bonds, offers to exchange U.S. Treasury bonds for shares in a state-owned company to ease its debt burden.

And what if that SOE is a company that has the next big thing in self-driving cars, and its stock price goes through the roof like Tesla's did?

The stock goes from \$10 to \$100 a share, and people, institutions, and countries holding U.S. Treasury bonds flock to swap them for shares of a state-owned company that, like you, is more profitable than U.S. Treasuries, right?

What happens if the \$100 stock price continues to soar to \$1,000, but then the SOE's technology turns out to be inferior to that of competitors like Tesla, and the company turns out to have no vision for the future, and the stock price plummets back to \$100, then \$10?

Even now, as part of a company's restructuring, the option to exchange bonds for stock is sometimes granted, but isn't it amazing that there were already people who had the idea of doing this on a national level, and history shows us the results and ramifications?

However, the reality is that with a national debt of over \$31 trillion and a Treasury bond balance of \$25 trillion, the size of the U.S. Treasury balance has become too large for the U.S. to exchange all of its \$25 trillion in Treasury bonds for equity.

As we can see from the fact that Apple, currently the number one stock market capitalization in the U.S., has a market capitalization of only \$2.6 trillion, and LG Energy Solutions, the number two stock market capitalization in South Korea, when it listed on the stock market, swept away the liquidity in the stock market, reducing the demand for other stocks and delaying the rise of the stock index, it seems impossible to implement such an equity conversion method in the modern era with major side effects and ramifications.

However, John Law's use of stock market speculation to solve the sovereign debt problem in the 18th century, when financial markets were underdeveloped, is controversial, but compared to Spain's inability to solve its excessive sovereign debt problem, which led to a moratorium, despite a massive influx of gold and silver from its Latin American colonies, John Law's idea seems ingenious.

However, John Law is still not immune from criticism as a fraudster because his stock bubble eventually ended in a crash, leaving many victims, and his history as a gambler is more suspect than his integrity as an economist.
One wonders what would have happened if the Mississippi Company had been able to capitalize on the Louisiana Territory's development rights, and had survived as a growth company rather than a bubble, providing dividends and investment gains to its investors.

The debate still rages over whether John Law was an economist and financier who wanted to enrich the economic lives of the common people by expanding the supply of non-convertible money, or whether he was an imitator and fraudster who, instead of creating stable income opportunities for the French aristocracy and solving the country's debt problem with his brilliant ideas, stole the money of countless failed investors.

The bursting of stock market bubbles is actually a classic financial event with a long history, as they have been occurring since the advent of the joint stock company.

When the Dutch and British East India Companies set sail and brought back spices and gems from their voyages through India and Southeast Asia, the stock prices of these companies skyrocketed.

However, investing in the stocks of these companies was a risky all-or-nothing proposition, as they often battled natural disasters such as typhoons and cyclones during their long voyages, and often did not return in one piece from battles with Islamic forces and indigenous peoples in the areas they traveled.

And the French and British bubbles mentioned earlier capitalized on vague fantasies of colonization in the Americas.

In their pitches to people who had never been to the New World, they claimed that the New World was full of precious metals such as gold and silver that were not common in Europe, and that kidnapping natives from Africa and selling them to Latin America would make them a fortune.

However, this vague and unproven revenue model proved to be unprofitable.

After Latin American countries gained independence in the 1820s, they turned to Europe to finance their shortfalls. The fantasy of Latin American countries made their government bonds popular in Europe.

Although the returns were unproven, the countries were rich in gold mines and other resources, so it seemed that they would soon become wealthy.

However, there were too many obstacles that prevented the vague revenue model from translating into solid returns, including political instability and corruption in Latin American countries and too many brokers in the middle.

Since the early to mid-19th century, the Industrial Revolution has created a boom in science and technology in the United Kingdom. In South Korea, the venture craze of the early 2000s led to a boom in investments in companies using the same technologies and ideas.

Among them, railroads led the boom in the commercialization of science, and there was a boom in the development of railroads and the establishment of railroad companies. Like the dot-com bubble of the 2000s in the United States, railroad companies proliferated, and their stocks and bonds sold like hotcakes.

But as the glut of railroads proved unprofitable, and the technology of the ventures turned out to be a pipe dream, the bubble began to deflate.
The same happened in the stock market boom before the Great Crash of 1929.
Ideas were everywhere, and technologies that looked like they could make a fortune if commercialized enticed investors. Thinking that the technology would change the future, investors jumped on board, and the scars of the tech bubble were devastating.

The history of stock market hype - that a technology is so good it will guarantee huge returns, or that a company is going to make a fortune by developing a gold mine, silver mine, oil field, or other resource, or that a company has found a treasure trove and needs investors to fund it - has been going on since the advent of the stock market, and it has always created bubbles.
And like a lie, the bubble always disappears without a trace, leaving only the victims who lost all their hard-earned money.

Stock market bubbles have a long history. If you look closely at the current bubble, you'll see similarities to past bubbles. The present is a repeat of the past, and the future is likely to be a repeat of the present and the past.

This book focuses on financial cases in the midst of a number of economic crises.
In the process of writing the book, the volume grew and was inevitably completed in four volumes. Part 1 begins with a general summary and organization of economic crisis cases, focusing on the basic background and knowledge to understand these cases.

Part 2 includes cases related to economic crises, from Tulip-mania in the Netherlands to the Florida land speculation bubble before the Great Depression of 1929, and adds representative financial fraud cases centered on Ponzi schemes.
Part 3 summarizes economic crises starting with the Great Depression of 1929, the bursting of the Japanese bubble in 1990, and the Asian financial crisis of 1997.

Part 4 covers South Korea's application for an IMF bailout in 1997, the global financial crisis of 2007, and the bankruptcy of Akegos Capital in 2021, and adds an overview of the psychological theories of speculation.

We believe that the stories of the bubbles caused by greed, and how we overcame the numerous financial and economic crises that followed, will provide many people with survival wisdom for the present and insights into how to deal with economic crises in an uncertain future.

Chapter 1

Understanding Money and the beginnings of speculation

Reflections on the economic crisis

1. Overview of the economic crisis

An economic crisis is a situation in which an economy experiences a severe downturn or disruption with negative consequences for individuals, businesses, and governments, such as high levels of unemployment, bankruptcies, financial market instability, declining GDP, inflation, or rising debt.

There are many factors that can cause an economic crisis, including financial imbalances, government policies, foreign currency shortages, bubble bursts, changes in global trade patterns, political turmoil, natural disasters, or other unexpected events.

The severity of an economic crisis can range from mild to severe, depending on the depth and duration of the recession.

So, can the recent bankruptcies of U.S. financial institutions Silicon Valley Bank, Signature Bank, and Silvergate Bank, as well as UBS's merger with Credit Suisse, be considered economic crises?

As will be mentioned in the discussion of economic crises below, there are many types of economic crises, such as financial institutions' bankruptcy directly resulting from the bursting of the real estate bubble, fiscal crises caused by excessive national debt, foreign exchange crises caused by foreign currency shortages, complex economic crises caused by accumulating trade imbalances, or general economic crises caused by political instability.

In addition, modern economic crises are often caused by a combination of several categories, and their remedies often require a combination of prescriptions.

However, by looking at past economic crises, we can find similarities to the current situation, and by looking at the outcomes and impacts of past crises, we can make some predictions about the outcomes of current measures.

In the case of the financial crisis, deregulation prior to the crisis has always been cited as one of the causes.

Many argue that this deregulation also contributed to the bankruptcies of Silicon Valley banks and others.

They point to the deregulation of Systemically Important Financial Institutions (SIFIs) as outlined in the Dodd-Frank Act, the strongest U.S. financial regulatory legislation enacted after the 2008 global financial crisis.

SIFIs are systemically important financial institutions. SIFIs are financial institutions that pose a threat to the stability of the financial system as a whole if they become insolvent or suffer from liquidity risk.

As such, they are considered to be very important to the financial markets and the economy as a whole, and are subject to strict regulation and supervision.

Those who argue that deregulation has contributed to the current crisis point to the law's designation of SIFIs as institutions with $50 billion or more in assets, which the Trump administration raised to more than $250 billion, leaving many mid- and large-sized institutions out of the loop.

Experts have argued that this deregulation has led to a deterioration in the liquidity and capital position of small and mid-sized banks, as many are no longer subject to strict capital requirements or supervision by the Federal Reserve.

2. A Review of Previous Economic Crises in the 20th Century

If we go back to the Dutch tulip mania that burst the first bubble, when the price of a single tulip was equivalent to the price of a whole house, there was a glut of tulips as people hoping to get rich from tulips started growing them. This glut drove down the price of tulips, and tulip investors lost big.

However, if we look a little deeper, the bubble in the price of tulips indicates that there was a lot of trading going on, and a lot of money, gold, and other means of commerce in circulation.

In modern terms, we could say that there was an oversupply of currency. This bubble would not have occurred if the Dutch had not developed commerce and trade due to their belief in heavy agriculture.

When the Netherlands gained its independence from Spain, many advocated mercantilism. As a result, foreign trade flourished, and capital flowed in from abroad.

Joint stock companies were established, private banks developed, the need for a central bank arose, and the need for an alternative to gold began to be recognized.

Revisiting the situation from a modern perspective, the oversupply of currency led to inflation, and while people today would invest in real estate, stocks, and coins, people back then invested in tulips.

If we had a monetary system managed by a central bank, as we do today, we would have tried to curb inflation by raising interest rates and reducing the money supply in order to bail out people who were suffering from excessive inflation.

However, the financial system was not yet developed, so it would have been left to the natural price adjustment function.

If you think about the principle that the price of a good is determined by supply and demand, the price of tulips will go up when they are in short supply and still have a scarcity value, and will naturally come down when the price goes up and people start growing them and there is a glut.

In a society with a developed financial system, commercial banks would have lent money to buyers using tulips as collateral, and investment banks would have pooled these loans and securitized them to create securitized securities such as Tulip-Backed Security (TBS).

They would also have divided the tulips into tiers 1, 2, and 3 based on the grade of the tulip, and created trenches by mixing mortgages on tier 3 tulips, which were bought by people with less money and less creditworthiness, with mortgages on tier 1 tulips, which were bought by people with more money and more creditworthiness.

They then create derivatives such as collateralized debt obligations (CDOs), which are debt-backed securities that are divided into senior, middle, and junior tranches based on the order of repayment, get a rating, and sell them to investors.

Insurance companies would have provided payment guarantees, such as credit default swaps (CDS), whether covering only corporations (like monoline) or individuals (like multiline), to help boost credit ratings.

Then, when the price of tulips plummeted due to an oversupply of tulips, borrowers with a 3 rating would have defaulted or declared bankruptcy. TBS, CDOs, and other derivatives would have cascaded downward, jeopardizing investment and commercial banks, and insurance companies would have suffered from claims on CDS.

However, at that time, the financial system was not as developed as it is today, so the collapse of financial institutions did not occur and a national economic crisis did not occur.

The same can be said for the bubble bursts of the French Mississippi Company and the British South Sea Company in the early 18th century.

However, these events were only possible because they were led by the state and transferred the burden of the state to the private sector, and because they were feudal dynasties, not democracies with elections like we have today.

War was an expensive affair, even in modern times and in the Middle Ages.

Wars that are not backed by economic power are unwinnable and always require more money than expected.

Even the United States, which remains the world's reserve currency and is the only country with the ability to print money, is burdened by the excessive fiscal debt that comes with an unlimited supply of dollars, so what about England and France in the Middle Ages?

With so much national debt due to frequent wars, England and France did not have a trust-based currency like the modern U.S. dollar.
Fortunately, it wasn't the globalized environment we have today, and because there were more domestic creditors than foreign creditors, it didn't lead to a major economic crisis.

However, the problem of excessive national debt, along with excessive interest payments, would have to be addressed at some point, and it was economists like John Rawls, who came to France from Scotland, who came up with a solution.

John Law wanted to issue a national currency that was not backed by precious metals such as gold or silver, which had value in their own right, but could circulate purely by the credit of the state. To accomplish this, he sought to establish a central bank and implement a system in which the central bank would control the supply of money through the power of issuance.

However, the economic climate at the time was such that the state was not yet trusted by investors, and frequent wars and political instability meant that gold and other alternatives were more trusted than state-issued currency.
The problem of inflation, a concern if the state were to print money without restriction, would also have been difficult to control under the system.

John Law solved the problem of national debt by capitalizing on the speculative sentiment of a stock bubble instead of the untrusted central bank-issued national currency.
The idea was to create an artificial bubble that would drive up the stock price of a corporation and exchange it for government bonds held by the private sector in a public offering.

In the process, John Law established a central bank and experimented with the possibility of a modern-day equivalent of a fiat currency (money that is not redeemable for gold).
Of course, this enterprise had to be created and given an interest by the state to create a rosy future, so the profits of a public company monopolizing a state-supported business could be believed to be guaranteed, even though they were not yet proven.
The name of this corporation was the Mississippi Company. The stock of this corporation, which held virtually all of the interests in the French government's colonial development projects, rose through the roof.
It was as if a modern-day manipulator had intervened in the stock market to drive up the price, offering to exchange the company's shares in a public offering

for French government bonds.

The French central bank issued money to lend working capital to a Mississippi company, and the Mississippi company issued shares to be exchanged for French government bonds from private investors.

In this process, there were two instruments that could be exchanged for the Mississippi stock: French government bonds and non-convertible money issued by the French central bank.

The currency issued by the French central bank was circulating in the market and could be exchanged for the Mississippi stock, and this currency acquired the status of not having to be redeemed for gold.

The French sovereign bonds that flowed into the Mississippi company could then be used by the Mississippi company to repay its loan to the French central bank, allowing the French central bank to issue additional notes backed by more sovereign bonds.

As Mississippi's stock price rose, private French government bonds flowed into Mississippi, and Mississippi used them to repay its loan to the French central bank, so that most of the privately held government bonds flowed into the French central bank.

The French government's debt to the private sector was transformed into debt to the French central bank, which is mostly owned by the French government. It was a process of internalization of debt.

The rise in the stock price of the Mississippi company and its initial public offering also resulted in an expansion of the money supply. John Law hoped that this would transform the French economy into a monetary economy, which would naturally expand the supply of the currency, which was in chronic shortage, and allow the economy to grow, including commerce.

Investors holding French government bonds knew that the Mississippi company's stock price had run wild, and they brought in their French government bonds, which were expected to be worth less, in exchange for the Mississippi company's stock, which was expected to be worth more.

By including notes issued by the French central bank in addition to French government bonds as a means of exchanging stock, the Mississippi company's stock was instrumental in bringing French banknotes, which had been discredited as irredeemable, into widespread circulation.

By the time most of the privately held French government bonds were exchanged for Mississippi stock, the stock price of the Mississippi Company began to plummet.

The company's stock was on its last legs as French aristocrats, well aware that the colony was not generating revenue, realized their profits.

Britain also followed the French bubble closely and artificially boosted its stock price through a company that traded slaves from Spanish colonies called the South Sea Company. The result was the collapse of the bubble.

However, the process of bubble bursting in these countries was to some extent a solution to the problem of national overindebtedness, and the damage was done to private investors.

After the chaotic 18th century, wars across Europe in the early 19th century, sparked by the Napoleonic Wars, led to the independence of Latin American countries that had been colonized by Spain and Portugal, and after the wars, the invention of the steam engine and the spinning wheel led to the Industrial Revolution in Europe.

Productivity increased, especially in the textile industry, and manufacturers were able to produce larger quantities of goods at a faster rate than ever before.

In addition, the railroad industry, which began with the invention of the steam engine, sparked a demand for investment funds in England and Switzerland, and private banks such as UBS and Credit Suisse began to be established to provide these funds.

Private banks, which were mainly engaged in private banking such as asset management for the wealthy, began to shift to corporate banking, which was established for large-scale financing such as investment in railroad projects.

In Europe and the United States, the rapid expansion of logistics infrastructure such as railroads and canals led to an oversupply of transportation capacity, which, combined with overinvestment and speculation in the sector, caused commodity prices and stock prices to plummet.

This led to a panic as financial institutions and related companies, such as railroads, went bankrupt and investors lost money due to defaults.

Panics caused by excess supply and overinvestment, such as the collapse of the bubble caused by investment in development projects in South America in the 1820s and the collapse of the railroad bubble in England in the 1840s, were caused by such excess supply and overinvestment.

At the time, the gold standard was being implemented in Europe, and due to the nature of the gold standard, government intervention in panics was limited.

The gold standard, which began to be adopted across Europe in the 19th century, starting with the United Kingdom, tied the amount of gold and the currency issued by the government to a fixed exchange rate, limiting the issuance of currency in excess of the gold reserves. This system caused deflation rather than inflation.

A financial system based on the gold standard allowed central banks and government authorities to take only a limited number of actions during economic crises, such as adjusting interest rates, by limiting the money supply based on gold reserves.

As a result, governments and central banks at the time could only wait for the market to resolve the problem through self-correction by the disappearance of the natural causes of the crisis or fluctuations in market prices, rather than taking measures such as various monetary policies or quantitative easing as in modern times.

However, due to the small size of the financial markets and limited excess supply, the ripple effects were often relatively mild.

In many cases, the market absorbed the oversupply in a staggered fashion, allowing prices to recover. As a result, the panics of the 19th century were often localized and relatively short-lived, and the downturns often passed naturally over time.

The governments and central banks of the time were often criticized by economists for their laissez-faire attitude toward the victims of economic crises, allowing the market to adjust itself even when panics occurred under the gold standard.

3. Reflections on the Great Depression of 1929

At the turn of the 20th century, World War I not only changed the face of warfare, but also demanded enormous war expenditures.

Countries like Britain, France, Germany, and Japan were unable to meet the rising costs of war and were forced to abandon the gold standard and increase the supply of money.

This increased amount of money caused severe inflation after the war ended. After the war, in order to fight inflation by reducing the supply of money and raising the value of their depreciated currencies, countries returned to the gold standard and sought to increase their gold reserves by raising interest rates.

The United States went so far as to outlaw private ownership of gold, attempting to keep it in the hands of the state. Countries like Germany, faced with the prospect of repaying huge war reparations as a defeated nation, sought to solve this problem by mobilizing the power of printing money.

However, like the hyperinflationary situation in modern-day Zimbabwe, with the value of the currency falling by the day and the cost of living rising by the day, German citizens were forced to stand in line with wheelbarrows full of German currency to buy bread.

It was also a time of humiliation for German currency, as thieves would steal the carts, leaving the money in the carts.

Germany's hyperinflationary period, when the country's central bank was hit hard and remains inflation-sensitive, is often cited as an example of the adverse effects of unlimited money printing using the power of fiat money.

The United States, the only country to emerge unscathed from World War I and one of the world's largest economies as it began to accumulate enormous wealth from the export of war materials, entered the prosperous 1920s with a real estate bubble in Florida, the development of the automobile, electronics, and aviation industries, and the emergence of new technologies such as mass production and management systems.

Despite the development of private banking, the Federal Reserve, established in 1913, did not yet have a complete system of control over financial institutions, and the U.S. federal government's economic laissez-faire approach emphasized minimal intervention in the economy, so bank loans were easily accessible without much regulation.

In the same way that optimism about the future seemed to rule the world during the dot-com bubble, optimism and expectations about the U.S. economy led to the use of leverage in stock trading, and the U.S. stock market boomed.

Leverage is when someone who doesn't have money uses the power of money to make a profit, such as when someone who wants to buy a $300,000 apartment only has $100,000 in their pocket and takes out a $200,000 loan to buy the house.

In the stock market, leverage was also contributing to the stock market bubble by inflating the size of transactions through credit. During the stock market boom, leverage in the market was allowed to be as high as 10x.
When you're leveraged and the price of an asset rises, you can make a lot of money because your costs are pretty much fixed, but if the price of the asset crashes, you're probably going to get a margin call.
The brokerage firm holding your shares as collateral will either have to sell them in a counter-trade, or pay more of your money as a deposit to keep them afloat.

The dangers of leveraged investing were demonstrated in the United States in 2021, when Korean-American Bill Huang bet heavily on Chinese tech stocks, using $10 billion of his own money and $40 billion in leverage, and lost nearly $20 billion in two days when the stock market crashed.

The incident, which earned Bill Huang a place in the Guinness Book of World Records for the largest loss in the shortest period of time, cost Credit Suisse, which had lent him the money, more than $5 billion, and was eventually acquired by UBS in 2023.
The U.S. stock market was turning from investment to speculation through these leveraged investments, and the flood of money was turning to real estate after the U.S. stock market.

Undeveloped areas such as Florida began to experience a development boom as the automobile industry and railroad extensions made them more accessible, and a surplus of money began to pour into these areas to invest in development projects, creating bubbles in real estate and stocks. Prior to the 1800s, the world was in a state of excess demand, where there was always a shortage of basic necessities to consume.

However, the increase in productivity due to the development of science and technology created enough supply to offset the excess demand, and now supply exceeded demand.

In the 19th century, there were several panics caused by excess supply, but they were localized and short-lived, caused by excess supply in specific sectors such as railroads, agriculture, and textiles.

Stock market crashes and financial institution failures also contributed to the magnitude of the panic, but there was little that governments or central banks could do under the gold standard, and over time, prices self-corrected and production fell back to pre-panic levels.

Was there a desensitization from the economic crises of the 19th century?

There were bubbles in a wide range of sectors, including excess supply in the commodity market, bubbles in the real estate market, expanding leverage in the financial market, and bubbles in the stock market, and the overheating of financial institutions that were investing in stocks was getting bigger and bigger, unlike the 19th century bubble.

However, people were still optimistic about the markets and the future, and that optimism would be shattered on a Tuesday in October 1929.

In commodity markets, inventories began to rise as consumer demand fell short of supply.

When the stock market crashed, individuals, companies, and financial institutions that had invested in stocks with leverage and credit were hit hard and began to fail.

Prior to the 20th century, the financial system was not yet mature, and certain events, such as bank runs, would cause some financial institutions to fail.

But now, thanks to the development of the financial system, the speed and impact of crises are much different.

The panic in the U.S. quickly spread to Europe due to increased trade between the U.S. and Europe, and countries around the world faced a global economic crisis.

Because this economic crisis was so different from previous ones, case analyses and prescriptions for past economic crises were not very effective, and economists had different opinions.

In the maelstrom of the Great Depression, protectionism such as tariff barriers and import quotas were prevalent to protect domestic industries, and under the gold standard, the supply of currency was limited, making it impossible to take policies such as quantitative easing, and trade was often restricted to prevent scarce gold from flowing out of the country.

Restrictions on the money supply under the gold standard caused deflation, while restrictions on foreign trade and protection of domestic industries by protectionism exacerbated the recession because there was no market for the excess supply of goods.

4. Overcoming the Great Depression
What Europe, Japan, and the United States have in common in overcoming the Great Depression is that they abandoned monetary tightening through the abolition of the gold standard and supplied money to the market through monetary expansion or fiscal expansion policies.

In the U.S., President Franklin D. Roosevelt implemented policies to increase demand through fiscal policies such as the New Deal, and expanded the money supply by abolishing the gold standard in 1933. However, it was not until World War II that the United States fully escaped the Great Depression.

Europe's recovery from the Great Depression was similar to that of the United States. Fiscal policy was used to stimulate private demand and the abolition of the gold standard to expand the money supply.

However, a complete exit from the Great Depression would have to wait until World War II.

Japan abandoned the gold standard in 1931 and expanded its money supply. The Japanese government chose to use its power to easily raise money in the government bond market.

It took control of the Bank of Japan to raise money directly from the bond market and used fiscal stimulus to pay for wars and increase government investment in infrastructure projects.

However, the currency was heavily overstretched from the Sino-Japanese War and other wars, so in the late 1930s, the government switched to a policy of strict monetary control to fight inflation.

It wasn't until the Great Depression that finance really began to have a major impact on the wider economy.

Under the gold standard, the money supply was limited, so it didn't cause inflation and there was never a problem with an excess supply of money. Therefore, the role of banks and financial institutions was very limited.

However, when it was necessary to expand the money supply in times of war or to overcome the Great Depression, the cumbersome gold standard was abandoned and credit was expanded through banks.

As banks became the center of frontline finance, acting as a bridge between the private sector and the government, the impact of their failure on the economy was significant.

After the end of World War II, the Bretton Woods system was introduced to address the problem of inflation, as the wartime expansion of the money supply caused inflation. The solution to inflation was to return to the gold standard.

The first step was to set a fixed exchange rate for gold and the dollar, while all other countries except the United States maintained a fixed exchange rate with the U.S. dollar.

Through this fixed exchange rate system, a stable exchange rate could be realized, and on that basis, international trade could be stabilized and international trade could be expanded. This was the moment when the U.S. dollar's position as an official reserve currency was guaranteed by the U.S. economic power.

5. Economic crises and responses after the gold standard was abandoned

Under the Bretton Woods system, the exchange rate between gold and the U.S. dollar was maintained for many years at a rate of $35 per ounce of gold.

However, due to the large U.S. trade deficit in the 1960s and the expansion of the supply of U.S. dollars to finance the Vietnam War, the U.S. abandoned the gold standard in 1971.

The price of gold, which had been pent up under the Bretton Woods system, skyrocketed, while the value of the dollar plummeted. At over $2,000 per ounce today, gold has increased in value 57 times in just over 50 years.

During the two oil shocks of the 1970s, it was popular to increase the value of money by raising interest rates to counter inflation caused by rising oil prices. However, Britain, which had lost its position as a world power to the United States after World War II, was losing its competitiveness in the global market, falling behind Japan and Germany.

The accumulation of trade deficits and inflation caused by the oil shocks depreciated its currency, the pound, and the government faced a fiscal crisis in the aftermath of expansionary fiscal policies to stimulate the economy. The outflow of dollars from the accumulating trade deficit led to a foreign exchange crisis, and the UK was forced to apply for a bailout from the IMF in 1976.

The UK's request for an IMF bailout was due to a combination of a fiscal crisis caused by fiscal policies to stimulate the economy and a trade and foreign exchange crisis caused by the depletion of foreign currency due to the accumulation of trade deficits.

In the late 1970s, the Jimmy Carter administration appointed Paul Volcker as chairman of the Federal Reserve to fight inflation. He was nicknamed the "inflation fighter," and he quickly raised the benchmark interest rate to nearly 20%.

Rising interest rates in the U.S. will increase the demand for dollars to invest in the U.S. from abroad, causing the dollar to strengthen and contributing to economic growth in manufacturing powerhouses such as Germany and Japan, which have a comparative advantage in export prices.

However, there is always a risk of an economic crisis in times of monetary tightening.

In the case of the U.S., the artificially high interest rates of 20% kept inflation under control, but the crisis came when the recession, especially the bursting of the real estate bubble, became a reality.

Forced to pay higher deposit rates to attract deposits in competition with commercial banks, U.S. savings and loan associations (S&Ls) began investing in risky products, such as oil fields in the North Sea and Mexico and high-yield commercial real estate, to improve their profitability.

They had to compete for high-interest deposits, forcing them to look for higher-yielding investments.

As the cost of leverage increased due to the high interest rate situation, and investors exited the real estate market due to the oversupply of commercial real estate and real estate tax reform, real estate prices plummeted, and savings and loan associations began to go bankrupt in 1988.

The collapse of financial institutions due to the bursting of real estate bubbles and the resulting financial crisis is a common case of economic crisis in the modern global economy. The financial crisis that occurred in the three Nordic countries in the 1990s was also caused by the failure of financial institutions due to the collapse of asset prices in real markets such as real estate.

The collapse of financial institutions following the bursting of real estate bubbles is recognized as a regular pattern in modern economies, with the Nordic financial crisis, the collapse of the Japanese bubble, and the 2008 global financial crisis being some of the most notable examples.

All of these preceding real estate bubbles started with deregulation and low interest rates, while bubble bursts are associated with factors such as rising interest rates, increased regulation, and overcapacity.
In addition to these factors, all of the above-mentioned financial crises had a large number of loans that exceeded 100% LTV (Loan to Value).

In the case of Japan, the high interest rate situation in the United States in the early 1980s caused the dollar to strengthen, and the remarkable growth of Japanese companies led to an annual trade surplus with the United States.
The United States, on the other hand, was hoping to resolve the so-called twin deficits by accumulating a fiscal deficit along with a trade deficit.
In 1985, the United States initiated the Plaza Accord to resolve the trade deficit problem politically.
The United States demanded that Japan, West Germany, and other major countries appreciate their currencies to improve their trade balances, and they agreed.

The appreciation of the yen by nearly half led to a decline in Japan's exports, and Japan, alarmed, adopted a policy of low interest rates and monetary easing to revitalize the economy through continued economic growth and domestic demand.

However, the released money flowed into the real estate and stock markets, creating a serious asset price bubble, and unlike West Germany, which, along with Japan, was subject to the Plaza Agreement's exchange rate appreciation and raised interest rates in 1987 in fear of an asset price bubble, the Japanese central bank thought that the price situation was stable and missed the time to intervene in the market to soften the economy.

Inflation was stabilizing due to falling import prices caused by the strong yen, so the government was tolerant of asset price bubbles.

However, in 1989, as the social problems caused by the bubble became serious and overheated, with loans of more than 100% LTV becoming widespread, various austerity and regulatory policies began to emerge, including the raising of interest rates by the central bank of Japan and restrictions on the total amount of loans to the real estate market.

The 1988 Bank of International Settlements (BIS) rule that banks must maintain a BIS ratio of 8% or higher also had an impact.

If a Japanese bank failed to maintain a BIS ratio of at least 8%, it would be designated as a failed bank, unable to participate in foreign exchange transactions, and expelled from international financial and trade markets.

In addition, when the Bank of International Settlements recommended that the Japanese government limit the total amount of loans to within 2.5 times equity capital to strengthen banks' asset quality, the newly appointed Bank of Japan governor Mieno tried to heal the asset price bubble and strengthen the asset quality of banks and other financial institutions by raising interest rates and restricting the total amount of loans.

The collapse of asset price bubbles in Japan's real estate market and stock market pushed the Japanese economy into recession, and as financial institutions became insolvent, the Japanese government took fiscal policy to stimulate the economy.

This was due to a traditionally reluctant business climate, interest groups that were too strong to attempt reforms such as labor reform, and concerns about increasing non-performing loans through monetary easing, all of which were addressed through fiscal policy rather than monetary policy.

In addition, fiscal policy was prioritized as a short-term solution due to the strong power of the Japanese Ministry of Finance, direct budget execution, and the ease of understanding spillover effects.

However, the Japanese government's fiscal policy has led to an increase in the supply of long-term government bonds and a decrease in the price of long-term government bonds, which in turn has led to an increase in long-term interest rates, weakening demand for real estate.

This had a negative impact on the real estate market and led to the accumulation of non-performing loans by Japanese financial institutions.

When financial institutions began to fail due to deteriorating overseas investments and defaults in the 1997 Asian currency crisis, the Japanese government belatedly tried to resolve the crisis by restructuring financial institutions, but it was too late to save them.

In order to stimulate the economy, the Abe administration has since implemented a policy of pumping money into the market through quantitative easing and government bond purchases of up to 80 trillion yen per year through the Bank of Japan.

Despite the fact that this QE has resulted in assets of the Japanese central bank exceeding 90% of GDP and government debt exceeding 200% of GDP, making Japan one of the most indebted countries in the world, the government's attempts to push inflation above 2% have not been successful.

The Bank of Japan, the country's central bank, moved from a zero interest rate policy to a negative interest rate policy and even used a yield curve control policy to control long-term interest rates, but Japan's recession and deflation were so severe that the target inflation rate of 2% was difficult to achieve.

The Nordic countries, on the other hand, had a different solution. The three Nordic countries faced a crisis when the real estate bubble burst, causing real estate values to halve and financial institutions to collapse under the weight of halved collateral values.

The financial authorities in these countries immediately infused public funds. Financial institutions that were likely to take time to turn around were nationalized to prevent the spread of damage to the private sector, and the government took the lead in restructuring.

While everyone's interpretation of what happened is different, and there are many variables, including differences in the environment and the size of economies, there have been crises that were resolved in a relatively short period of time with the right policies at the right time, and others that were prolonged by misjudging the timing, causes, and opportunities for market intervention.

The bursting of the U.S. dot-com bubble in the early 2000s is a similar example of a financial crisis, albeit of a different kind.

Instead of real estate, it was investments in stocks of dot-com companies that were grossly overvalued relative to their intrinsic value that caused the bubble to burst, resulting in losses and a crisis for the financial institutions that invested in these companies.

Real estate bubbles start with a positive environment for real estate purchases, such as deregulation through financial liberalization measures and tax reform, and an expansion of the money supply, which leads to inflation. During a bubble, there is an oversupply of real estate, which eventually leads to a tulip-mania-like situation.

However, in less developed financial systems, such as those prior to the 20th century, the problem-solving process could be delayed as they tried to rely on the self-correcting behavior of supply and demand.

However, in modern economies, where inflation is tightly controlled through intervention and supervision by monetary authorities, the government can quickly intervene in the market by raising interest rates and restricting lending.

Raising the cost of leverage through interest rate hikes and monetary tightening accelerates the bursting of bubbles by encouraging supply and demand to self-correct.

The Korean savings bank crisis can be understood in a similar context.
During the real estate boom, savings banks increased their share of real estate PF loans to earn high returns, but when the real estate market turned downward as the Bank of Korea raised interest rates to curb inflation, savings banks began to fail.

6. Asian Financial Crises since the 1990s
If financial crises are the most common form of economic crises, foreign exchange crises are economic crises that are victimized by hegemonic rivalries between countries.

In particular, developing countries tend to have a large outflow of dollars depending on interest rates in the U.S., and when the U.S. raises interest rates, developing countries often experience foreign exchange crises due to the influx of dollars into the U.S.

The Asian economic crisis in 1997 had many complex factors, but it can be considered a foreign exchange crisis in that the country applied for a bailout from international financial organizations such as the IMF due to a lack of foreign exchange.

A foreign exchange crisis is a crisis caused by a shortage of foreign currency, which is mainly caused by the accumulation of foreign currency outflows due to trade deficits and fluctuations in the exchange rates of competing countries that cause trade imbalances.
In particular, the fact that these countries had taken measures to liberalize the international movement of capital prior to the crisis is also pointed out as a cause of the crisis.

Measures to liberalize international capital flows are a major feature of modern economic crises, and when countries with restrictive policies such as protectionist trade policies open their domestic capital markets through capital liberalization measures, their domestic markets are often robbed due to weak domestic financial conditions.

In addition, there are many cases where the exchange rate system does not properly reflect the true intrinsic value of the market due to a rigid exchange rate system such as a fixed exchange rate system, a market-managed average exchange rate system, or a peg to the U.S. dollar, resulting in a foreign exchange crisis due to attacks by hedge funds.
This is not only a problem for developing countries, but can also occur in

developed countries with well-developed financial systems.

A good example is the 1992 currency crisis in the United Kingdom, which had to manage its exchange rate in a narrow band against the German mark in order to join the eurozone's fixed exchange rate system called the European Exchange Rate Mechanism (ERM).

Compared to Germany, which had a high-interest rate policy to counter inflation in the former East Germany after reunification, the U.K. failed to defend its exchange rate against attacks from hedge funds that saw the pound as overvalued relative to its intrinsic market value. As a result, the U.K. was forced to leave the ERM and abandon the euro.

Southeast Asian countries were competing fiercely with a rising China in global markets in the mid-to-late 1990s.
In early 1994, China, which was running a trade deficit, abruptly devalued its currency by 49.8%, from 5.82 yuan to 8.72 yuan per dollar, when the gap between its official exchange rate, the fair rate, and the market rate nearly doubled, and its trade balance subsequently turned into a surplus.

This triggered trade deficit in China's Southeast Asian competitors and meant foreign currency outflows.

Despite the outflow of foreign currency, countries such as Thailand, which was using a rigid dollar peg, should have devalued its currency, the baht, but due to the rigidity of the exchange rate system, the baht was not devalued and remained overvalued by being linked to the dollar.

As a result, the value of the baht plummeted due to capital outflows from overseas investors and attacks on the baht by speculators, and the Thai government tried to maintain the value of the baht by selling dollars in the market to defend it, but it only depleted its foreign exchange reserves.

In South Korea, the exchange rate of the yen against the dollar was heavily influenced by Japan's competitors in the global market.
When the yen appreciated through the Plaza Agreement in 1985, Korea began to expand its exports in the global market.

The appreciation of the yen led to years of booming growth for the South Korean economy. In the process, South Korean companies over-borrowed to get bigger, and their debt-to-equity ratio reached 400% before the crisis, making them a potential risk.

In addition, financial and foreign exchange liberalization measures were taken in stages to join the OECD, and the government's desire to appreciate rather than devalue the currency in order to achieve a GDP per capita of $20,000 also played a role in distorting the value of the won in the market.

However, in 1995, there was a growing sentiment in the U.S. and elsewhere that the Japanese economy needed to be revitalized due to the excessive yen and the Great Kobe Earthquake.
In response, the yen began to depreciate against the dollar through the reverse plaza agreement, and South Korea recorded its worst trade deficit in 1996.

Despite this outflow of foreign currency, South Korea operated a rigid exchange rate regime called the market-managed average exchange rate.
Despite the outflow of foreign currency through the trade deficit, South Korea's domestic currency, the won, was overvalued due to the rigid exchange rate regime, which did not reflect its intrinsic value.

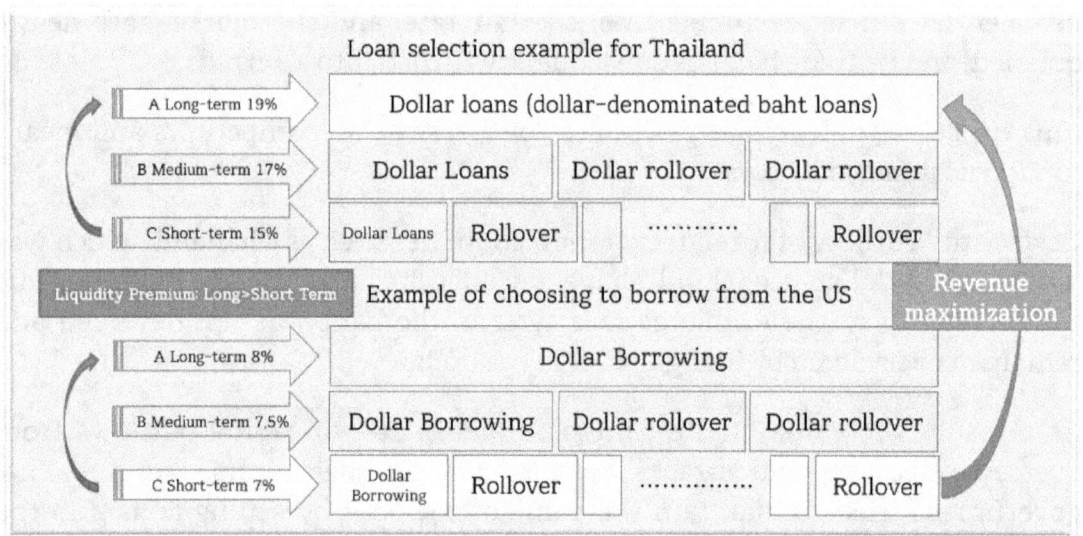

The potential risks were compounded by the so-called "carry trade," in which financial firms engaged in international foreign exchange financing transactions borrowed short-term foreign debt with the lowest interest rates to maximize yields and invested in long-term loans or risky instruments with the highest interest rates in Southeast Asia, such as Thailand.

A series of bankruptcies of large companies starting in early 1997 and the accelerated withdrawal of dollars from South Korea, triggered by Thailand's currency crisis in July 1997, led to a sharp decline in South Korea's foreign exchange reserves.

General financial companies, which had sought to maximize their margin through carry trades, began to withdraw domestic funds in large numbers as they faced difficulties with the suspension of short-term foreign debt extensions and defaults on Thai investment funds.

News of bankruptcies of Korean conglomerates began to emerge in early 1997, and the stock market plummeted. The exchange rate reached a record high of over 2,000 won to the dollar, and interest rates exceeded 20%.

In December 1997, South Korea officially announced its application for an IMF bailout, and with the promise of $55 billion in foreign exchange, the government embarked on the restructuring required by the IMF.

7. Economic Crisis in the Post-2000s
The economic crises since 2000 have had wider ramifications due to globalization, increasing global imbalances, and the sophistication and complexity of financial techniques due to the development of science and technology.

As global financial markets became increasingly complex and interconnected, financial technology was forced to become more advanced, and financial experts devised new ways to hedge risks, making financial markets more complex.

However, the use of these new financial techniques also contributed to the economic crisis after 2000, as the use of derivatives allowed investors to take on large amounts of leverage and risk, which contributed to the collapse of financial institutions during the 2008 global financial crisis.

A hedge fund called LTCM made an ambitious entry into global capital markets in the 1990s, recruiting stars like Robert Merton and Myron Scholes, who developed the famous Black-Scholes Model of option pricing theory, as partners.

Despite their sophisticated and complex econometric models using expensive computers, they were forced to file for bankruptcy in 1998 when a Russian moratorium caused the price of Russian government bonds they invested in to plummet.

Prior to that, in 1995, Nick Leeson, who worked in the Singapore office of Barings Bank, was engaged in derivatives trading, selling straddle options and buying futures contracts on the Nikkei 225 index.
He had been losing money on his derivatives trades for years, but concealed his

losses by keeping them in a secret error account called 88888.

However, he had a substantial long position in futures, and when the Great Kobe Earthquake in Japan caused massive losses, he faxed his resignation to the London headquarters and admitted his losses.
The consequences of this single individual's behavior were devastating, leading to the collapse of the 200+ year old Barings Bank of England.

Despite these derivative-induced market crises, derivatives continued to be introduced to the market, reflecting the theory of portfolio diversification, the idea that risk can be lowered by combining portfolios with low correlation coefficients.

Asset-backed securities (ABS), mortgage-backed securities (MBS), collateralized debt obligations (CDOs), and collateralized mortgage obligations (CMOs) were developed to securitize loans, and investors believed that these products would hedge their risk and minimize their losses.

After the Great Depression in 1929, the repeal of the Glass-Steagall Act, which prohibited U.S. banks from investing customer deposits in risky assets such as stocks, allowed investment banks to enter the business of commercial banks and led to the creation of large financial institutions through mergers.

In the U.S., where deposit interest was capped by Regulation-Q, which was enacted after the Great Depression to prevent bank runs, the relaxation of Regulation-Q led to increased competition for deposits and the need for financial institutions to find and manage higher yielding investment opportunities.

In the early to mid-2000s, the U.S. real estate market began to gradually increase in price as the Federal Reserve kept interest rates low to stimulate the U.S. economy, which had been depressed by the bursting of the dot-com bubble and the events of September 11, due to lower leverage costs, a growing U.S. population, and a growing desire for homeownership.

The influx of money into the real estate market also spurred speculative demand, causing home prices to soar and demand for development to increase. In order to finance the high-demand real estate market, real estate lenders began to relax their lending standards and offer subprime mortgages to borrowers with lower credit scores and higher risk weights, leading to overheating.

In the international market, international capital, such as sovereign wealth funds and pension funds in the Middle East, which had accumulated wealth as oil prices rose due to increased demand for oil from China and India, which were continuing to grow at a high rate, began to seek safe-haven assets.

In this atmosphere, U.S. investment banks began to develop derivatives that could diversify risk based on advanced financial techniques and receive superior credit ratings through payment guarantees from large insurance companies such as AIG, and focused on the booming U.S. real estate market.

Subprime mortgages were pooled with higher-rated prime and alt-A mortgages into securitized securities called MBS, which were divided into classes called tranches based on creditworthiness, risk, and profitability, and issued as CDOs, which are a mix of stocks and other instruments, or CMOs, which are just mortgage products.

Credit rating agencies assigned ratings to each security, and CDOs and CMOs with high ratings were considered safe because they hedged risk through diversification.

But derivatives like CMOs and CDOs, which were created using complex securitization techniques, and subprime mortgages, which were poorly documented and therefore less creditworthy, were difficult to value properly.

As the real estate market overheated and inflation occurred, interest rates were raised, as they always are, and monetary policy was tightened to control inflation and bring the U.S. economy back to a soft landing. From 2004 to 2006, the Federal Reserve raised interest rates from 1% to 5.25%.

As real estate prices fell due to the oversupply of real estate and rising interest rates, subprime mortgage borrowers who took out loans with high interest rates began to default on their loans, and foreclosures on homes increased, causing real estate to fall even further.

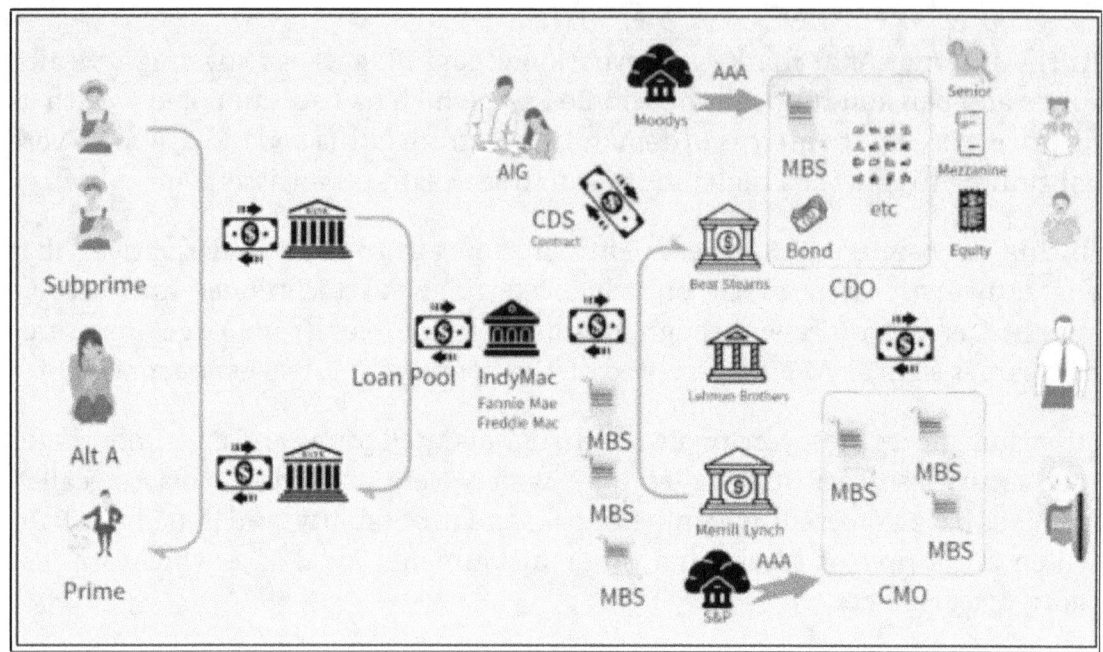

Subprime mortgage borrowers, in particular, often had adjustable-rate loans, which made rising interest rates more costly for them and led to more bankruptcies. As subprime mortgages defaulted, investors in related derivatives such as MBS, CDOs, and CMOs began to lose money in a cascading fashion.

In 2007, subprime mortgage lender New Century Financial went bankrupt, triggering the global financial crisis. In March 2008, Bear Stearns Bank, the fifth largest U.S. investment bank, collapsed, and that summer, the largest U.S. mortgage lenders - IndyMac, Fannie Mae, and Freddie Mac - were shut down.

Then, in September 2008, Lehman Brothers, the fourth largest U.S. investment bank, collapsed, and Merrill Lynch, the third largest, was sold to BOA. The world's largest insurance company, American International Group (AIG), was injected with public funds.

In 2009, GM, the world's largest automaker, filed for bankruptcy, and the U.S. government directly injected $2.81 trillion into the crisis.

The total GDP of South Korea is about $1.8 trillion, and the total GDP of France, the seventh largest economy in the world, is about $2.8 trillion, so the U.S. government injected more money than the total GDP of France at that time.

During the GFC, the market for mortgage products was about $13.1 trillion in 2007, and while not all of them failed and lost money, the investment banks that had fun with MBS, CDOs, etc. during the real estate boom suffered the most.

They had contracted a lot of CDS, an insurance-like product, to cover the risk of mortgage products, but they could not expect to be paid back by the insolvent insurance companies.

When subprime mortgages went bad, commercial banks and New Century Financial, which were the frontline lenders and originators of MBS, went bankrupt first, and companies such as IndyMac, Fannie Mae, and Freddie Mac, which primarily pooled mortgages and created securities called MBS, went bankrupt second as MBS went bad.

In addition, investment banks such as Bear Stearns, Lehman Brothers, and Merrill Lynch, which supplied MBS products to create other derivatives such as CDOs and CMOs and sold them to investors, filed for bankruptcy due to the failure of CDOs and other derivatives.

AIG, the world's largest insurance company, had been making a killing selling CDS to hedge against the failure of these derivatives, but it also filed for bankruptcy as it was inundated with requests to fulfill CDS contracts due to the cascading failure of MBS, CDOs, CMOs, etc.

Bernanke, then chairman of the U.S. Federal Reserve, was an expert on the Great Depression and the Japanese economy, and an expert on quantitative easing.

Believing that the prescription for the global financial crisis was monetary expansion, including quantitative easing, which injects money into markets, including financial institutions and corporations, he cut the benchmark interest rate to near zero in addition to injecting public money.

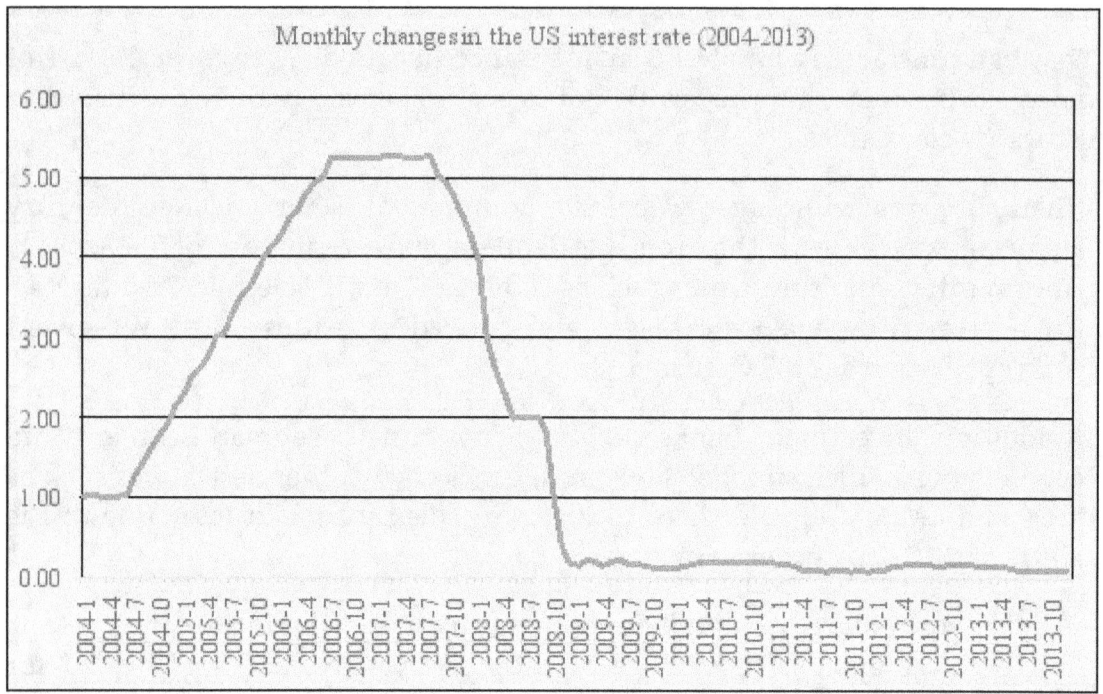

As money was injected into the market through quantitative easing - the purchase of Treasury securities in the secondary market - as well as public money injections and interest rate cuts, financial institutions and companies that were on the verge of bankruptcy were saved and the U.S. economy began to recover.

In addition, the economic crisis in the U.S. triggered the fiscal crisis in Greece, which spread to other southern European countries, including the so-called PIGS (Portugal, Italy, Greece, and Spain).

In order to prevent the spread of the global financial crisis, the United States emphasized the global economic coordination system through economic communities such as the G20, and helped each country prevent foreign exchange crises through the supply of U.S. dollars such as the U.S. dollar currency swap agreement.

8. Characteristics and Prospects of Modern Economic Crises

We have reviewed the major examples of economic crises throughout history. Let's look at the commonalities between these examples and consider what makes modern and previous crises different and what has changed.

As we've seen, globalization and financial sophistication were the keywords that distinguished the 20th century from the pre-20th century. While there had been European powers that had practiced mercantilism and free trade before, there was not yet an international marketplace that included most of the world's countries.

With the exception of a few countries, such as Spain, the Netherlands, and the United Kingdom, the ratio of domestic to international trade was overwhelmingly in favor of the domestic market, and international trade was low.

Since the supply of money was not smooth due to the gold standard or silver standard system that was implicitly used as the country's monetary system, resolving excess demand in the real economy was always a problem, and international trade was mentioned as a measure to expand supply to solve this problem.

Therefore, under the gold standard, a financial crisis was unlikely to occur due to a shortage of money supply, and a foreign exchange crisis was unlikely due to restrictions on international trade and cross-border capital movements.

The economic crisis at that time was a fiscal crisis, a problem of government bonds issued by the state to finance the war expenses, mostly due to frequent wars.

The fiscal crisis led to several bubbles that burst as a result of the excessive transfer of government debt to private investors. However, the biggest temptation for governments to solve excessive government debt is to print money using their unlimited printing presses.

In order to do this, the cumbersome gold standard had to be abolished, and until 1971, the gold standard was on and off the table.

Because of the limited amount of gold, the supply of money based on gold reserves has always been limited, and except for the influx of gold from Spain's colonization of Latin America, gold has always been scarce, limiting the supply of currency.

In a market economy, there is always a shortage of money and always a shortage of real goods, so both the real and money markets are in a state of excess demand. Say's law, which states that supply will meet all of its own demands, was a statement of economic conditions at the time.

This closure to international trade and capital transactions limited the scope of the crisis and helped keep it localized.

In addition, government intervention, such as the abolition of the gold standard, artificial issuance of government bonds, and indiscriminate printing of money, was the cause of all economic problems.

Therefore, the role of the government was limited and criticized for its intervention in the market, and the role of the government was reduced.

During Spain's heyday of colonization, more than 80% of the world's gold and silver poured into Spain, but due to its many wars, it was surprisingly Spain that declared the first national moratorium in the 16th century.

The large supply of gold and silver from its colonies led to inflation, as did the expulsion of Jews and confiscation of their property to pay for the war effort.

Nevertheless, war expenses were always insufficient, so they borrowed from European financiers and issued various government bonds, but the pressure of accumulated debt and interest was considerable enough to declare a moratorium.

Once mercantilism was advocated after the Age of Exploration, the importance of international trade was emphasized, and the concept of balance of payments was recognized.

In addition, the system of finance began to work in earnest to manage money such as gold and silver that came from the trade surplus.

In the 19th century, the capitalist economy, which had always suffered from excess demand and believed in Say's law, solved it through the industrial revolution and created a unique situation of excess supply.

As railroads spread as a means of transportation, private banks were established to finance the massive investment, and the financial system began to expand from personal to corporate finance.

The word credit is used interchangeably in the financial world with loans, credit, and the use of leverage.

In addition, the issuance of national currencies that appeared after the gold standard was also based on credit, so credit expansion is used to mean the expansion of the money supply.

As transactions increased, it became necessary to introduce a convenient currency rather than inconvenient currencies such as gold and silver, and as the interests of the government, which wanted to issue money based on government trust, coincided, central banks for money issuance began to be created.

And as the number of private banks that intermediated between the central bank and the private sector increased, the system of finance began to take hold.

As credit expanded through finance, many people used leverage to make investments, and as monetary expansion led to inflation, some argued for a strict gold standard to limit inflation.

However, war is an urgent and exigent situation that is often accompanied by measures that restrict freedom, such as martial law. The need to pay for war through the abolition of the gold standard took precedence over concerns about inflation.

World War I was a major milestone in the modern era and the era before it.

Previously localized wars were joined by allies and allies, and countries in Europe, Asia, and the Americas all participated in the war, and cross-border trade began to flourish, and capital began to be traded through a modernized financial system.

Unlike in the past, when economic crises were localized, wars spread around the world, and economic crises began to spread quickly, as did inflation. Globalization and financial sophistication had begun.

In the United States, where the surplus in the international trade balance due to the supply of war materials brought in gold from abroad and expanded the supply of money, inflation occurred due to the excess supply of money in the money market. The money went into real estate and the stock market, and the market boomed.

The financial market and the real market became closely interconnected as the financial system supported the real market, and the financial market and the real market became closely interconnected as the financial system supported the real market.

Underlying the spread and prolonged nature of the new economic crisis of the Great Depression were changing trends of globalization and financial sophistication.

The price of goods and services, and the price of money, and hence interest rates, are all based on prices in the domestic market, but they are also valued higher and lower according to an international standard called the exchange rate. The exchange rate is a variable that operates within the market economy system by allowing the market to self-correct and converge imbalances to equilibrium.

When a surplus in the capital account occurs through a surplus in the international trade balance or an increase in domestic interest rates, the supply of foreign currency, such as inflowed dollars, increases, causing the price of foreign currency to decrease and the price of the local currency to increase, resulting in an appreciation.

In the opposite case, a trade deficit causes a devaluation. When the value of the domestic currency changes, it has a self-correcting function that leads to changes in the trade balance or capital account through changes in price competitiveness and returns to equilibrium.

However, in the past, there have been restrictions and price controls on international trade and capital movements, such as the introduction of protective tariffs or quotas, foreign exchange regulations, and rigid foreign exchange systems such as the peg system, such as the confrontation between mercantilism and mercantilism and protectionism and liberalism, and these regulations have been used as a means to prevent the spread of economic crises.

In the wave of globalization, it has become impossible for countries to survive unless they open their doors to the world, and in order to receive international support such as joining international organizations and providing loans, they have no choice but to participate in the global market competition system by opening their capital markets, introducing free trade, and abolishing anti-market price control policies.

In the past, the economic system was rigid due to the gold standard and various regulatory policies, so the frequency of economic crises was low, and it took time to overcome economic crises.

However, in the modern era, globalization and financial sophistication have accelerated the speed of global spread and ripple effects.

As global connectivity has also increased, countries have been affected by economic crises in each continent of the world, and the frequency of economic crises affecting their countries, whether large or small, has increased, but they are often overcome in a relatively short period of time due to cooperation between countries and the elasticity of market prices.

However, the increase in connectivity due to globalization has led to a prolonged cycle of economic crises, including the spread of economic crises and the triggering of other economic crises.

Even if it is difficult to see it as an inherent cause, the propagation of external economic crises while having internal problems often bursts bubbles or acts as a trigger for crises.

In addition, the development of financial engineering has led to the development of complex hedging techniques for various risks in financial markets.

These techniques are increasingly distancing investors from the underlying assets and layering the process of cause and effect, making it increasingly difficult to determine the market size of related products, their spillover effects, and their causes.

The development of more complex and data-driven financial instruments, coupled with recent advances in artificial intelligence and science and technology, is likely to continue, and it is difficult to predict which crises will manifest themselves as side effects of this financial sophistication.

Since World War I and the Great Depression, the pace of globalization has accelerated, and financial techniques have become increasingly sophisticated. As a result, economic crises are expected to become more frequent.
Just as it's easy to get a prescription for a known illness, such as a cold or a body ache, the prescription for a known economic crisis can be easily identified by looking at past examples.

However, like diseases that have not been fully conquered or whose causes are difficult to identify, such as cancer or the coronavirus, economic crises that occur when the market economy system fails or cannot keep up with the pace of globalization and financial sophistication are likely to be more difficult to overcome.
Before the 20th century, excess demand was a common sense situation, and excess supply was a special event that only occurred in exceptional cases.

In the 20th century, however, excess supply became the norm, and the Great Depression hit the world.
It took time to find a solution to this new form of economic crisis, and it was

only after the extreme and destructive events of World War II that the Great Depression was fully healed.

No one knows what the future holds for science and technology.
Attaching eyeballs to teddy bears, one of the most labor-intensive side jobs in backward countries 30-40 years ago, is still done in Bangladesh and other parts of Asia and Africa, but with the rise of A.I. technology, these simple repetitive tasks are being transformed into forms such as A.I. data labeling.

While there may not seem to be much difference in essence, computerized tasks have a preconceived notion of being technology-intensive and seem luxurious to the uninitiated.
Sooner or later, people who glue eyeballs to teddy bears will be able to make better money labeling A.I. data on computers, and there's no telling what even simple repetitive tasks will look like in 10 years.
In this changing world, it is difficult to predict what kind of finance will come out in the next 10 years and what kind of speculative products will become an issue in the real world.

We don't know if the current global financial order based on the gold standard and the dollar will be reorganized around other currencies, or if it will be centered on digital assets such as Bitcoin.
If systems like Decentralized Finance (DeFi) become mainstream, many financial institutions and intermediaries may disappear.

In addition, due to the complexity of IT-based systems, new and unforeseen variables, such as market disruptions by computer hackers or the stability of computer systems, can trigger economic crises.
As new types of economic crises arise from different sources, will the world's central banks be able to prevent them through conventional methods such as monetary policy and quantitative easing programs that buy government bonds in the secondary market?

However, in order to survive, we need to keep up with the development of new technologies and prepare for the risks they bring and how to deal with them.
It is also necessary to study and prepare for economic crises that will occur in a similar form to the existing ones, as they are likely to occur now or in the near future.

The concept and origins of finance

The concept of finance has evolved over time into both classical and modern meanings. In the classical sense, finance refers to the management of money and assets to generate financial returns.

This includes raising money through equity investments and loans to achieve specific goals, such as financing a project or investing in a business.

In the modern sense, finance has expanded to encompass a broader range of activities, including financial planning, risk management, and financial engineering.

Financial planning involves creating a comprehensive financial strategy, including retirement planning, investment management, and tax planning.

Risk management involves identifying and assessing potential financial risks and developing strategies to hedge and manage those risks.

A specific example of finance is the stock market, where investors buy and sell shares of companies. Here, companies raise money by selling shares, and investors can profit from the increase in the price of the shares.

Another example is a bank loan, where a borrower can access funds to finance a project or purchase, but must pay interest along with the principal.

Concepts like budgeting, saving, and investing can also be applied to personal financial activities.

For example, individuals create a budget to manage their income and expenses. They can also save money for future goals, such as buying a home, and invest in stocks or mutual funds to grow their wealth over time.

Finance plays an important role in modern society by providing individuals, businesses, and governments with the tools and resources they need to effectively manage their finances.

The origins of finance can be traced back to ancient civilizations like Mesopotamia and Egypt. In these early societies, finance played an important role in facilitating trade and commerce and managing resources and wealth.

In one of the earliest civilizations, Mesopotamia in the Middle East, finance emerged as a means to facilitate trade and commerce.

For example, the Babylonians developed a financial system of loans, credit, and guarantees, as well as contracts and promissory notes, to help merchants finance their ventures and manage risk.

The ancient Babylonians had an advanced system of lending and credit for their time. This is evidenced by various cuneiform tablets found by archaeologists in modern-day Iraq.

One of the tablets, known as the Murashu Documents, reveals details about the financial behavior of Babylonian merchants. The Murashu family was a prominent merchant family in Babylon in the 5th century BC, and these documents provide a record of how they ran their business.

According to these records, the Murashu family provided loans to other merchants and collected interest on the loans. They also used a contract called a "kudurru" to secure these loans.

A kudurru is a type of ancient clay tablet used to record a legal agreement or contract between two parties, and kudurru were considered sacred objects that symbolized the presence of a god or goddess.
The kuduru would summarize the terms of the agreement, and both parties would add their seals or signatures to it, and then it would be kept in a temple or other sacred place.

By creating a kuduru, the parties involved invoked the power of the gods to ensure that the contract was honored. Violating the terms of a kuduru contract was considered a serious offense against the gods and could result in divine punishment. The kuduru served as a contract or promissory note in the modern sense.

In addition to lending, the Murashu family also engaged in a form of business known as pardes, a joint venture with other merchants to finance large trade expeditions or other ventures.

Babylonian finance was very sophisticated for its time, and the records left behind by merchants like the Murashu family give us a sense of this complex system and how it was managed.

In ancient Egypt, finance played a very important role in managing the country's resources and wealth. Pharaohs and other rulers developed systems to finance their armies, temples, and public works, and they also developed sophisticated financial systems that included loans, deposits, and guarantees.

Records of ancient Egyptian finance are primarily found in papyrus scrolls discovered by archaeologists. These documents reveal how the Egyptians managed their finances and the various tools they used to do so.

One of the most important tools in the ancient Egyptian financial system was the shat. Shats were government bonds sold to the private sector to finance public projects. Shats promised a fixed interest rate and were issued in a variety of denominations to make them accessible to a wide range of investors.

Another financial instrument was the banking system, called per-ankh. Per-ankh means "house of life" and was a bank that offered a variety of financial services, including loans, deposits, and guarantees. Per-ankh was associated with temples and managed by priests who worked there.

In addition to these tools, the ancient Egyptians developed sophisticated accounting and record-keeping systems.
They used hieroglyphics and shorthand symbols to record transactions and kept detailed records of taxes, tributes, and other sources of income.

Over time, finance continued to evolve and become more sophisticated. During the Middle Ages and Renaissance, European merchants and bankers developed new financial instruments to finance trade and commerce.
During the Middle Ages and Renaissance, European merchants and bankers played a pivotal role in financing long-distance trade and commerce.

They developed new financial instruments and techniques to manage risk, raise capital, and facilitate international trade, one of which was the bond.
Bonds were essentially loans from investors to governments, merchants, or other organizations. Bonds promised a fixed rate of interest and were issued for a set period of time, after which the principal was repaid to the investor.
Bonds were a way for governments and merchants to finance projects, and they were an attractive investment for individuals looking for a stable source of income.

The development of bonds in Europe is closely linked to the emergence of the modern banking system.

In the 14th and 15th centuries, Italian merchants and bankers began to develop new financial instruments such as bills of exchange and bills of exchange. These financial instruments allowed merchants to finance long-distance trade and commerce by reducing the risks associated with currency exchange and transportation.

Records from this period reveal information about the development of bonds and other financial instruments.
For example, the records of the Medici Bank, one of the most important banks of the Renaissance, reveal how bonds contributed to the financing of merchants and governments, and how they were used.

The Medici Bank was founded in Florence, Italy, in the 14th century and grew rapidly. It played an important role in financing the activities of the Florentine government and the papacy, as well as providing funds to merchants engaged in long-distance trade.

The records of the Medici Bank contain information about the bonds issued by the bank and their interest rates, as well as information about the various projects financed through bonds, including the construction of public buildings and military financing.

The development of bonds and other financial instruments during the Middle Ages and Renaissance played an important role in the growth of international trade and commerce.
The concept of modern finance emerged during the Industrial Revolution, a period of rapid technological and economic change that began in the late 18th century and continued into the 19th century.

One of the main factors that led to the development of modern finance during this period was the development of large-scale manufacturing. As large-scale factories began to replace small workshops and handicraft production, new sources of capital were needed to finance the construction of factories and the purchase of machinery.

This led to the development of new financial instruments such as private bonds and stocks that could be sold to investors to raise capital.

Another factor in the development of modern finance during this period was the growth of transportation infrastructure. The expansion of railroads and other modes of transportation created new opportunities for trade and commerce, but also new risks. To manage these risks, new forms of insurance and credit were developed, such as marine insurance and letters of credit.

Records from this period contain a wealth of information about the development of modern finance. For example, the records of the Bank of England, which was founded in 1694 but played a central role in the development of modern finance during the Industrial Revolution, reveal how financial institutions evolved during this period.

One specific example in the Bank of England's records that demonstrates the development of finance during the Industrial Revolution is the growth of joint stock companies. Joint stock companies were a new type of business organization that allowed investors to buy and sell shares of ownership in a company, providing a way for ventures to raise large amounts of capital.

Banks in the UK played a key role in the development of joint stock companies by providing a safe and reliable place for investors to deposit their money.

This helped build trust and faith in the financial system and made it easier for joint-stock companies to raise capital through the sale of shares.

The Bank of England played an important role in financing the Industrial Revolution by providing loans to manufacturers and issuing government bonds to finance public works projects.

The Bank also played an important role in the development of the stock market by providing liquidity and stability to the market. The development of modern finance during the Industrial Revolution laid the foundation for the growth of the financial industry.

Overall, the concept of finance has evolved from funding in the classical sense to include a wide range of activities and services that are critical to the functioning of modern economies. In addition, the rapid pace of technological innovation has led to the emergence of new financial products, strategies, and systems that have changed the way financial markets operate.

In recent years, as financial institutions have grown larger and more interconnected, the complexity of finance has also increased, increasing the risk of systemic failure and market disruption.

In addition, the use of leverage and derivatives has increased, making the financial system more difficult to understand and manage.

Advances in computer power and data analytics have led to the development of sophisticated algorithms and quantitative models that enable financial professionals to analyze large amounts of data and make better-informed investment decisions, while the rise of blockchain technology and cryptocurrencies have opened up new avenues for financial transactions and investment opportunities.

The increasing use of data analytics and artificial intelligence for investment decisions and risk management will continue, and the growth of decentralized finance (DeFi) and other blockchain-based financial systems may further disintermediate the financial industry.

Decentralized finance (DeFi) is a financial system built on blockchain networks, such as Ethereum, that enables peer-to-peer transactions without intermediaries such as banks or other financial institutions. In a decentralized financial system, financial transactions are executed using smart contracts, which are self-executing programs that automatically execute transactions based on predetermined conditions.

In the traditional financial system, intermediaries play an important role in facilitating transactions between parties. Banks acted as intermediaries between borrowers and lenders, executing money transactions and managing the associated risks.

In decentralized finance (DeFi), however, intermediaries can be replaced by programmatic code, as financial transactions are executed automatically through smart contracts powered by blockchain technology. This has the potential to remove many intermediary steps from the financial industry, making transactions faster, cheaper, and more efficient.

For example, in the traditional financial system, a borrower may need several intermediaries to get a loan, including a bank, a credit bureau, and a loan servicer, but in a DeFi system, a borrower can get a loan directly from a lender through a smart contract without any intermediaries.

The growth of DeFi and other blockchain-based financial systems could lead to greater levels of disintermediation in the financial industry as financial transactions become more automated and are executed directly between parties.

However, as the financial system becomes more complex, it will also become more important that regulatory and supervisory systems keep pace with these changes and provide adequate oversight to prevent systemic risk.

Establishment and development of banks

The first modern bank is generally recognized as the Bank of Venice, founded in 1157 in Venice, Italy.
The founder of the Bank of Venice is unknown, but it is believed to have been established by wealthy Venetian merchants and bankers.

Its original purpose was to provide a safe place for merchants to deposit money and do business, and to provide credit to finance trade and commerce.
To provide credit is to make a creditor's capital available to a debtor for a period of time based on the debtor's creditworthiness, which is a broader definition of credit than that used by financial institutions, including loans, payment guarantees, discounting of commercial paper, and leasing.

The bank was located in Venice's central marketplace, Rialto Square, which gave it easy access to merchants from all over the world.
It was also strategically located near the city's main harbor and waterways, so it could play an important role in facilitating trade and commerce.
Over time, the Bank of Venice became increasingly influential and played an important role in the city's economic and political affairs.
It provided loans and credit to the Venetian government and played a major role in financing the city's wars and other military campaigns.

The Bank of Venice's influence extended far beyond Venice and Italy. The bank helped spur economic growth and development in Venice. The bank attracted merchants and traders from all over the world, making the city a major financial center.

The Bank of Venice also served as a model for other banks and financial institutions in Europe, helping to build the modern banking system that exists today.
Its legacy can be seen in the continued importance of finance and banking in the global economy, as well as in the development of banking customs and institutions throughout Europe and the world.

It was not until the 17th century that banks began to emerge as institutions for the safety of money and the facilitation of trade, and the first modern bank is considered to be the Bank of Amsterdam, founded in 1609.

The establishment of a bank in the city was driven by several factors, including the need for a stable means of financing trade and commerce, the desire to promote economic growth and development in the city, and the need for a stable and reliable currency.

The founder of the Bank of Amsterdam was the city of Amsterdam, which established the bank as a public institution. Its original purpose was to provide a safe and reliable place for merchants to deposit their money and do business.

The bank also played an important role in promoting the city's economic growth and development, financing major infrastructure projects, and supporting new industries and businesses.

One of the key features of the Bank of Amsterdam was the use of a stable and reliable currency known as the Bank Guilder.

This currency was issued based on the amount of gold and silver the bank held, which helped ensure its stability and reliability. The bank also provided credit to finance trade and commerce and to support government projects.

Over time, the Bank of Amsterdam became increasingly powerful and influential, playing an important role in the city's economic and political affairs. This helped to establish Amsterdam as a major financial center, attracting merchants and traders from all over the world.

The bank's reputation for stability and reliability also helped establish the Dutch guilder as one of the most trusted and widely used currencies in Europe. The bank's development helped to fuel Amsterdam's economic growth and development and establish it as a major financial center. It also helped establish a modern banking system that focused on stability and the use of a reliable currency.

Today, the Bank of Amsterdam no longer operates, having merged with other Dutch banks in the late 20th century.
However, the bank's legacy can be seen in the development of modern banking practices and institutions.

After the Bank of Amsterdam was founded in the early 17th century, the Bank of England was established in 1694 in response to the financial crisis and instability that plagued England in the late 17th century.
Prior to its creation, England lacked a central bank or monetary authority, making it difficult to manage the country's finances and maintain a stable currency.
The Bank of England was founded by a group of wealthy merchants and bankers led by William Patterson, who proposed the creation of a national bank to help stabilize the country's finances and provide a reliable currency.

The bank was granted a royal charter by William III in 1694 and was authorized to issue banknotes, lend to the government, and regulate the money supply.
One of the Bank of England's main features was its ability to lend to the government, which helped support Britain's wars and other expenses.
This gave the bank considerable influence over the government, as well as the country's economy and financial system.
As the Bank of England's influence grew, London became a major financial center of the world, attracting merchants and traders from around the globe.
Founded in 1694, the Bank of England began as a private bank, but as the bank of the Crown, it also served as the central bank.

In 1844, the Bank of England Act granted it the exclusive right to issue money in England and Wales, and in 1946, it was nationalized and officially recognized as a central bank.

Today, the Bank of England remains the central institution of the United Kingdom's financial system, responsible for managing the country's monetary policy and ensuring the stability and credibility of its currency.
Since the 18th century, many countries have established banks to finance their growing economies and support international trade.

These banks were often founded by governments or wealthy individuals, and their primary goal was to provide loans and credit to businesses and individuals.

One important development in banking during this time was the rise of joint-stock companies, which allowed investors to pool their capital and share in the profits and losses of the business. This profit model helped create larger and more stable banks, as well as spurring greater investment and economic growth.

In Europe, many countries established their national banks during the 18th and 19th centuries.
The Bank of France was founded in 1800 to help finance the Napoleonic Wars and support economic growth. Similarly, Deutsche Bank was founded in 1957 to help stabilize the German economy after World War II.

They financed economic growth and development, facilitated international trade, and helped build currency stability and confidence. In addition to national banks, the 18th and 19th centuries also saw the rise of private banks founded by wealthy individuals.

These banks played an important role in financing industrialization and other economic developments, as well as fostering greater investment and innovation.

These European private banks, founded in the 18th and 19th centuries, have a long and storied history. Here are some specific examples of private banks founded in Europe in the 18th and 19th centuries that are still famous today.
Rothschild & Co
Mayer Amschel Rothschild started his banking business in Frankfurt, Germany, in 1798. He had five sons, who later established branches in London, Paris, Vienna, Naples, and Frankfurt.

The London branch, founded by Nathan Mayer Rothschild in London in 1811, became the foundation of today's Rothschild & Co. Nathan Mayer Rothschild was the third son of Mayer Amchell Rothschild.

Rothschild & Co. initially focused on providing banking and financial services to European aristocracy and royalty, but over the years expanded to other European countries, including France, Austria, and England.
The bank played a key role in financing major infrastructure projects, such as the construction of railroads and canals.

In the late 19th and early 20th centuries, Rothschild & Co had a presence in many parts of the world, including the United States and South America. The bank continued to provide financial services to wealthy individuals as well as governments and corporations.

In the 20th century, Rothschild & Co. diversified beyond traditional banking and finance. It established a commercial banking division and expanded into asset management, private equity, and other financial services.

Today, Rothschild & Co is a leading global financial services firm, providing a wide range of services to governments, corporations, and wealthy individuals. The bank operates in more than 40 countries and is recognized for its expertise in mergers and acquisitions, debt and equity financing, and asset management.

BNP Paribas (BNP)

BNP Paribas was founded in 1822 as the Banque Nationale de Paris (BNP) in response to the need for a state-owned bank to finance the growth of the French economy.

Initially focused on providing banking services to businesses and individuals in France, in the late 19th and early 20th centuries BNP expanded beyond France to other parts of Europe, including Belgium, Italy, and Spain, and to other parts of the world, including Africa and Asia.

Then, in 1999, BNP merged with French investment bank and financial services company Paribas. This merger created BNP Paribas, one of the largest banks in Europe.

In the 21st century, BNP Paribas diversified beyond traditional banking and finance. It established a wealth management division and expanded into asset management, insurance, and other financial services.

In recent years, BNP Paribas has focused on sustainability and corporate responsibility.

The bank engages in various activities to promote sustainable development, including financing renewable energy projects and supporting social and environmental issues.

Coots & Co

Coots & Co was founded in London in 1670 as a goldsmith and silversmith.

The company began offering banking services to wealthy clients in the 18th century, and over time became known as a premier private bank.

In the 20th century, Kutz & Co began to expand its services beyond traditional banking to include wealth management and investment services. The bank built a reputation for personalized service and discretion to meet the needs of wealthy individuals and families.

In 1996, Coates & Co merged with National Westminster Bank (NatWest), one of the UK's leading banks.

However, in 2010, Coates & Co was acquired by Spanish bank Banco Santander. Despite the changes in ownership and the banking industry as a whole, Coates & Co has remained focused on providing personalized service to its clients.

The bank has maintained its reputation as a premier private bank catering to the needs of high net worth individuals and families.

Credit Suisse

Credit Suisse is a Swiss bank that was founded in 1856. It began as a partnership between Alfred Escher and several other investors.

The bank began as a local lender to finance the expansion of the Swiss railroad network, but quickly grew to become one of the largest banks in Switzerland.

In the early 20th century, Credit Suisse began expanding into international markets, opening branches in London, New York, and other major financial centers.

The bank offered a wide range of services to corporate and institutional clients and established itself as a leader in the global banking industry.

In the 1990s, Credit Suisse began to diversify its services, expanding into investment banking, wealth management, and asset management.

The bank acquired several financial institutions, including investment bank First Boston and Swiss private bank Clariden Leu.

Like many other banks, Credit Suisse faced significant challenges during the 2008-2009 global financial crisis.

The bank weathered the crisis by reducing its exposure to risky assets and focusing on its core strengths in investment banking and wealth management.

Today, Credit Suisse is one of the world's largest banks, with operations in more than 50 countries and more than 45,000 employees.

However, it was unable to overcome the aftermath of major investment losses in 2021 and was acquired by UBS in 2023, ending its nearly 170-year history.

Union Bank of Switzerland (UBS)

UBS was formed in 1998 by the merger of the Union Bank of Switzerland (UBS), founded in 1862, and the Swiss Bank Corporation (SBC), founded in 1872.

The Union Bank of Switzerland (UBS) was formed in 1862 through the merger of two existing banks, the Winterthur Bank and the Toggenburger Bank. The Winterthur Bank was founded in 1860 by Swiss businessman Georg Fischer and Swiss psychiatrist and economist Ludwig Binswanger.

Toggenburger Bank was founded in 1861 by Swiss banker and politician Johann Jakob Ritter.

The Swiss Bank (SBC) was founded in 1872 by Swiss politician, entrepreneur, and railroad pioneer Alfred Escher.

Escher was a key figure in the development of Switzerland's infrastructure in the 19th century, including the construction of the Gotthard railroad tunnel, and he saw the need for a private Swiss bank to finance these projects and support the country's economic growth.

The Swiss bank has grown to become one of the largest banks in Switzerland, with a focus on investment banking and global finance.

The merger of UBS and SBC created one of the world's largest banks focused on investment banking and wealth management.

The new bank was named UBS AG (Union Bank of Switzerland Aktiengesellschaft) and was headquartered in Zurich, Switzerland. Today, UBS is a global financial services company with operations in more than 50 countries and is one of the largest banks in the world.

The first national bank in the United States was established by Congress in 1791 under the first Secretary of the Treasury, Alexander Hamilton. The bank aimed to finance the new government and promote economic growth and stability.

The main controversy surrounding the bank was whether the federal government had the authority to create such a bank.

Opponents, led by Thomas Jefferson and James Madison, argued that the Constitution did not give Congress the power to establish a central bank.

They believed the federal government would give the bank too much power and threaten the sovereignty of the states.

Supporters of the bank, led by Alexander Hamilton, argued that the Constitution did give Congress the power to create a bank.

They believed the bank would help stabilize the economy, manage government finances, and provide a stable currency. Despite this opposition, the National Bank was established and operated for 20 years. However, in 1811, its charter expired and it was dissolved.

With the goal of stabilizing the nation's finances and supporting economic growth, the Second Bank of the United States was established in 1816 and played an important role in supporting westward expansion and the growth of industrialization.
This time, due to political pressures and disagreements over the bank's purpose and power, the bank was eventually dissolved in 1836.

Throughout the rest of the 19th and early 20th centuries, many private banks emerged as important players in the U.S. economy, one of the most famous being J.P. Morgan & Co, founded by financier J.P. Morgan.
In the late 19th century, Morgan's bank played an important role in financing industrialization and supporting economic growth, becoming one of the most powerful financial institutions in the United States.

There have been several large private banks in the United States since the 18th century, and here are a few examples of them.
JPMorgan Chase (JPMorgan Chase)
JPMorgan Chase is one of the largest banks in the world with over $3 trillion in assets. JP Morgan was formed in 2000 through the merger of JP Morgan & Co. and Chase Manhattan Corporation.

Chase Manhattan Bank was founded in 1799 by Aaron Burr, then Vice President of the United States, and a group of investors. The bank's original name was the

Manhattan Company.

Aaron Burr founded the company with the primary purpose of providing safe and reliable drinking water to the growing city of New York, but it quickly expanded into banking services, and by the mid-1800s it was one of the largest and most prominent banks in the United States.

The Manhattan Company merged with the Manhattan Company Bank in 1955 to become Chase Manhattan Bank.

JP Morgan & Co. was founded in 1871 by prominent American financier and banker John Pierpont Morgan, who had already made a name for himself in the financial world by advising and financing some of the largest industries of the time, including railroads and steel companies.

J.P. Morgan & Co. quickly became one of the most powerful and influential banking and investment firms in the world, playing a key role in financing the growth of the American economy in the late 19th and early 20th centuries.

The firm was involved in numerous high-profile transactions, including the financing of the U.S. Steel Company, the largest corporation in the world at the time.

John Pierpont Morgan was known for his ability to use his extensive network of contacts to bring investors and companies together to make large-scale deals and transactions. He was also a key figure in the creation of the Federal Reserve Bank in 1913, which was established to regulate the U.S. banking system.

JP Morgan & Co. continued to grow and expand, becoming a major player in the global financial services industry. The company was involved in several important mergers and acquisitions, including the 1959 purchase of the Guaranty Trust Company, which created the largest bank in the world at the time.

In 2000, the company merged with Chase Manhattan Corporation to form JPMorgan Chase & Co. today, one of the largest financial services companies in the world.

The merger of Chase Manhattan Bank and JP Morgan & Co. was the largest bank merger in history at the time.

The merger leveraged the strengths of both companies, including Chase Manhattan's retail banking and JPMorgan's investment banking capabilities, to offer a more comprehensive range of financial products and services.

Goldman Sachs

Goldman Sachs was founded in 1869 by German immigrants Marcus Goldman and his son-in-law Samuel Sachs.

It initially operated a small commercial paper business in New York, but soon began expanding into other areas of finance, including investment banking and wealth management.

In the early 20th century, Goldman Sachs became one of the leading underwriters of securities in the United States and played a key role in financing the growth of major industrial companies such as Sears, Roebuck & Co. and Ford Motor Company.

In the 1930s and 1940s, Goldman Sachs became a major player in corporate finance with a focus on mergers and acquisitions, financing the formation of several major companies, including IBM and GE.

In the 1970s and 1980s, Goldman Sachs expanded internationally, opening offices in London, Tokyo, and other major financial centers around the world. It also expanded its product offerings by establishing its own private equity and asset management divisions.

In the 1990s, Goldman Sachs was recognized for its expertise in technology and internet-related investments, playing a key role in the dot-com boom of the late 1990s.

It was also known for its ability to navigate volatile markets, earning a reputation as one of the world's most successful and profitable investment banks.

In the years since, Goldman Sachs has continued to evolve and adapt to changing market conditions. It overcame the global financial crisis of 2008 to emerge as one of the world's strongest and most stable financial institutions.

Morgan Stanley

Morgan Stanley was founded in 1935 when Henry S. Morgan and Harold Stanley left J.P. Morgan to start an investment bank. At the time of its founding, the Glass-Steagall Act was in effect in the United States, which distinguished between commercial and investment banking.

The Glass-Steagall Act strictly separated commercial and investment banking, so JPMorgan was founded as a commercial bank and Morgan Stanley as an investment bank.

Morgan Stanley initially focused on securities trading and underwriting, and quickly became a major player in the global financial services industry. In the 1950s and 1960s, the firm expanded into a broad range of investment banking and corporate finance services, including mergers and acquisitions, securities offerings, and other strategic advisory services.

In the 1970s, Morgan Stanley became the first Wall Street firm to enter Europe, opening offices in London and other major financial centers.

In the 1980s, Morgan Stanley played a major role in the merger and acquisition boom of the time, advising on several high-profile deals, including the leveraged buyout of RJR Nabisco.

It also became a major player in emerging markets, establishing a presence in Asia and elsewhere.

In the years since, Morgan Stanley has continued to evolve and adapt to changing market conditions. It overcame the global financial crisis of 2008 to emerge as one of the world's strongest and most stable financial institutions.

Citigroup

Citigroup is a multinational financial services company that provides a range of banking, investment, and insurance services to clients around the world.

The company was formed in 1998 through the merger of Citicorp and Travelers Group, and is now one of the largest banks in the world with over $2 trillion in assets. Citigroup has a long and complex history, having undergone several mergers and acquisitions over the years.

Citicorp was founded in 1812 as the Bank of the City of New York and became one of the largest banks in the United States. The bank was renamed Citibank in 1976 and is now the retail banking arm of Citigroup.

The Travelers Group was founded in 1864 as an insurance company. Over the years, it expanded into other financial services, including investment banking and wealth management.

In 1997, Travelers Group acquired Salomon Brothers, a leading investment banking and trading firm.

In 1998, Citicorp and Travelers Group announced a merger, creating Citigroup, one of the world's largest financial services companies.

The merger was controversial at the time because it involved combining a commercial bank and an insurance company, which was not allowed under existing regulations.

After the merger, Citigroup continued to expand its business lines and geographic reach.

It acquired several financial services companies, including investment bank Smith Barney and credit card company Associates First Capital.

Citigroup was heavily impacted by the 2008 financial crisis, which led to massive losses and government intervention.

Over the next few years, the company went through a series of restructurings and divestitures to focus on its core business and improve its financial performance.

Today, Citigroup is one of the world's largest financial services companies, operating in more than 160 countries and offering a wide range of financial services, including retail and commercial banking, investment banking, wealth management, and insurance.

In the early 20th century, many major national banks were established to provide a stable and flexible monetary system for the United States, including the Federal Reserve, which was created in 1913.

The Federal Reserve has played a key role in stabilizing the U.S. economy during times of crisis and promoting economic growth and stability.

After World War II, major banks such as Citibank and Chase Manhattan Bank emerged as major players in the global financial system.

They played an important role in financing international trade and investment and helped build the modern global financial system.

In recent decades, the U.S. banking system has undergone significant changes due to the consolidation of many smaller banks into larger institutions and the rise of new technologies such as online banking and mobile payments.

The establishment of major U.S. national and private banks has had a significant impact on the national economy and the global financial system, helping to promote growth and stability and supporting international trade and investment.

FRB, (Federal Reserve Bank)

The Federal Reserve Bank of the United States (FRB) is the central bank of the United States. The Federal Reserve System is called the Federal Reserve System (FRS), sometimes abbreviated as Fed. While the term Fed refers to the Federal Reserve System, it often refers to the decision-making body, the Board of Governors of the Federal Reserve System, as it refers to the programs implemented by the Board of Governors.

The Federal Reserve System is commonly known as a three-pronged system: the 12 regional Federal Reserve Banks, the central Federal Reserve Bank in Washington, D.C., and the Federal Reserve Board, the decision-making body, and the Federal Open Market Committee (FOMC), which meets eight times a year to discuss and determine short-term monetary and financial policy.

The Fed was founded in 1913 in response to a financial panic and the need for a more stable banking system. The Fed has since played an important role in the U.S. economy and financial system, as well as the global economy. The Federal Reserve System was established by the Federal Reserve Act, signed by President Woodrow Wilson.
The act created a system of 12 regional Federal Reserve Banks, each with its own board of governors and a Federal Reserve Bank in Washington, D.C. The board of governors is composed of seven directors under a chairman.

The Board of Governors consists of a chairman and seven members, appointed by the president and confirmed by the Senate.
The president appoints a chairman and vice chairman from among the directors.
Directors serve 14-year terms, and the Chairman and Vice Chairman serve four-year terms.

The Chairman of the Federal Reserve is appointed by the President, but he or she exercises monetary policy authority, including setting interest rates, completely independently.

The Chairman of the Federal Reserve is often referred to as the President of the World Economy and has a strong global influence on financial policy.

While the Board's primary duties are to regulate credit conditions and oversee the Federal Reserve Banks, it also sets short-term monetary and financial policy through the Federal Open Market Committee (FOMC), which meets eight times a year in odd-numbered months (January, March, May, July, September, and November) and in June and December.

The FOMC has a total of 19 members, 12 of whom are eligible to vote. The seven members of the Board of Governors of the Federal Reserve System, the President of the Federal Reserve Bank of New York, and four of the regional Federal Reserve Bank presidents serve on a rotating basis and have voting privileges.

The remaining seven regional Federal Reserve Bank presidents who have not been appointed as members may attend meetings as non-voting members of the FOMC.

Because all members of the Federal Reserve System are voting members of the FOMC, the Fed is often confused with the policy or direction that the FOMC decides on, but it's safe to say that the FOMC's decisions are the Fed's decisions because it has a majority of the votes.

In particular, eight times a year, the FOMC releases to the media a post-meeting statement on the key interest rate, a dot plot (released at the March, June, September, and December meetings) that aggregates the projections of the 19 FOMC members on future interest rates, and a press conference with a Q&A with the Chairman of the Federal Reserve.

In addition to disclosing the current benchmark interest rate, the dot plot shows the upper and lower bounds of future interest rates and the direction of policy in the press conference of the Federal Reserve Chairman, which has a significant impact on the global economy.

The FRB is authorized to set interest rates, including the rediscount rate (the lending rate between central banks and commercial banks), purchase and issue U.S. Treasury securities (U.S. government bonds) (open market operations), and determine the reserve requirement ratio.

The FRB also publishes the "Beige Book" eight times a year, which is written by the president of each regional bank and synthesizes the opinions of leading businessmen, economists, market experts, and others on economic conditions.

The reason for having 12 regional banks was to allow the Federal Reserve to provide a more regionalized approach to monetary policy in different parts of the country.

The 12 regions were selected based on population and economic factors when the Federal Reserve Act was passed, and this decentralized structure allows for a broader range of voices and perspectives to be represented in the Federal Reserve's decision-making process.

Each Federal Reserve Bank is owned by member banks in its region, which are primarily commercial banks, which hold stock in each Federal Reserve Bank. However, the shareholders of the Federal Reserve Banks do not give them control over the policies or operations of the Federal Reserve System.

The Federal Reserve System is a decentralized central banking system that is not owned by any one entity or individual and consists of 12 regional Federal Reserve Banks located in major cities across the United States.

The 12 regional Federal Reserve Banks are
Federal Reserve Banks of Boston, New York, Philadelphia, Cleveland, Richmond, Atlanta, Chicago, St. Louis, Minneapolis, Kansas City, Dallas, and San Francisco.
.

The Fed has several core responsibilities: conducting monetary policy to stabilize prices and maximize employment, supervising and regulating banks and other financial institutions, and providing financial services to the U.S. government, foreign central banks, and other institutions.

One important function of the Fed is to conduct monetary policy. This involves setting interest rates and adjusting the money supply to promote economic stability and growth.
The Fed's policy decisions can have a major impact on the U.S. and global economy and financial markets.
The Fed also plays a key role in regulating and supervising banks and other financial institutions. It works to ensure the safety and soundness of the financial system and to protect consumers and investors.

The Fed also provides a variety of financial services to the U.S. government, foreign central banks, and other organizations, such as processing payments and maintaining the stability of the financial system. It can influence interest rates, inflation, and employment, among other economic indicators.
The Fed's role in regulating banks and other financial institutions has helped promote a more stable and resilient financial system, and financial services facilitate commerce and trade.

Because its policy decisions can affect global financial markets and economies, the Fed's influence extends beyond the United States.
Central banks around the world look to the Fed as a model for monetary policy and banking regulation.

The continued globalization of financial markets and the increasing complexity of the financial system present new challenges for the Fed and may require new approaches and tools to implement monetary policy and regulate financial institutions.

Monetary Systems and Central Banks

Looking back at how banks were founded and grew, they started out privately to provide credit to merchants in the course of their commerce and trade, but after the Middle Ages, there was a boom in the establishment of central banks led by governments and other public institutions.

These were established by governments as a solution to the problem of government debt under the gold standard. To understand this, we need to look at the question of monetary systems and monetary policy.

The modern monetary system is based on trust in the state and is sustained by the state's guarantee of payment for money that has no value in itself. In other words, the money in circulation today is strongly characterized as a guarantee that the state will pay its face value.

In the past, people who were uncomfortable with the lack of a medium of exchange in the barter economy began to pay attention to precious metals that were valuable and beautiful in their own right, among which gold, a rare and precious metal, has been with mankind for a long time.

As a rare and precious metal that does not corrode easily, is durable, and can be easily separated and transported, it is easy to distinguish from other metals and is difficult to counterfeit, making it suitable for money as a medium of exchange.

In particular, the introduction of a monetary system became necessary to collect taxes as centralized governments were established and taxation became a major source of revenue.

A medium such as money was needed to facilitate the collection of taxes and to ensure that the collected taxes retained their value and were liquid when needed.

In addition to gold, silver and copper were also circulated as money, but they did not reach the popularity of gold.

However, as the size of the economy grew and international trade became more active, the demand for money increased, and the supply of gold could not be increased rapidly due to its limited reserves, resulting in a state of excess demand, which was solved with suboptimal tools such as silver.

Some governments have tried to replace gold and silver with government-issued currency.

However, government credit did not seem to be more valuable than gold and silver, which had their own value.

Nowadays, the concept of nation and state is so well established around the world that it makes sense that a state would not honor its promises, but in Europe, the concept of nation was not created until the 18th and 19th centuries, so the idea of a nation or state was unbelievable at the time.

For example, let's go back a few hundred years from present-day New York to the New York of the past. If I had a piece of local currency backed by an American Indian chief, or a Dutch bill backed by the Dutch government, and New York came under Dutch control, and then came under British control, what would my bill be worth?

This is a very extreme example, but government guarantees of payment can vary in value depending on regime change, war, natural disasters, and other variables, and in the worst case scenario, they could be worthless pieces of paper.

However, if you had it in gold, you wouldn't have to worry about whether it was American Indian, Dutch, British, or whoever was ruling, which is why a currency that has its own value, like a gold coin, would be prioritized over government-issued money.

In Europe, wars between nations occurred one after another in the Middle Ages, and the demand for national currency increased due to various expenses required for warfare.
Due to the increasing cost of war, governments wanted to issue currency such as gold coins, but the limited amount of gold was not enough to meet the government's needs.

In desperation, governments issued bonds that were guaranteed to be paid by the state, which allowed them to borrow money from the private sector to pay for the war.

However, as governments overextended themselves, they were saddled with unaffordable debt and interest payments.

The common sense solution would be for governments to print money indefinitely to pay off their debts, but the money issued by heavily indebted and unreliable governments was nothing more than a piece of paper.

So government officials came up with the idea that if people didn't trust the government's guarantee because it wasn't trustworthy, they would trust it if they could show them gold and exchange it for gold, i.e., if it was a form of money backed by gold, and this evolved into the gold standard, the gold standard, and the gold exchange policy, which means that gold is the basis of the value of money.

For example, the British government shows people that it has a ton of gold in its vaults and promises to exchange a £1,000 note for a gram of gold.
If people can take a £1,000 note and exchange it for a gram of gold at any time, then the note has the same value as the gold. This assumes, of course, that the government fulfills its promise of exchange.

In such a situation, the government would be able to issue 1,000 X 1,000,000 = 1,000,000,000 pounds of money, since the amount of gold held by the government is 1 ton.

This puts a cap on the money supply, and it can't grow indefinitely.
If the government wants to increase the money supply, it has to mine, buy, or borrow more gold, so the money supply is limited.

Pure money backed by the government, which people did not trust, was replaced by government-issued money backed by gold, which people trusted, and the supply of money was limited, causing deflation.
Once the government adopted the gold standard, it could issue money, so it established a central bank as the issuing authority, and the central bank was responsible not only for issuing money but also for managing the government bonds issued by the government.

Governments, eager to escape the burden of mounting debt and sovereign debt issuance, placed the solution to their massive government debt on the central bank.

Central banks can often meet government demand by printing money in excess of their gold reserves, but this has the side effect of fueling inflation.

In the 18th century, as the sovereign debt problems of France and England became more severe, the idea was to transfer government debt to the private sector by exchanging government bonds for shares in stock companies instead of exchanging the bonds for scarce gold.

Then, the project to solve the government debt problem by exchanging the government bonds held by the private sector for shares of a corporation created by the private sector or the government.

Redeeming government bonds with money was only possible because of the gold backing behind the money, the existence of gold, and in order for government bonds to be exchanged for something other than money or gold, they had to be valuable in themselves, such as gold.

In order for government bonds to be exchanged for stock in a corporation, the stock in the corporation had to be worth something, and to do that, the value of the stock had to rise.

This process creates bubbles, and the inevitable collapse of these artificially created bubbles creates a lot of casualties, such as the stock bubble collapse of the Mississippi Company in France and the South Sea Company in the UK.

Governments and central banks have long dreamed of a system where the money they issue is backed by a cumbersome gold backing and can be printed indefinitely.

However, under the gold standard, which requires gold reserves to be greater than the supply of money, there is a limit to the amount of gold that can be printed, and the amount of money that can be printed cannot exceed that limit. In the modern era, major developed countries, including the United States, which could not manage the supply of money under the gold standard as its economy grew larger and larger, and the demand for money surged due to major wars, began to abandon the gold standard, and a credit society was established in which all transactions are carried out using government-backed money.

The government's ability to issue unlimited amounts of money has been a long-standing desire, but currently only the United States, the world's leading currency, is able to do so.

There are many economic variables to consider, such as inflation, asset price bubbles, and the devaluation of the Korean won in the international foreign exchange market due to overcapacity, if the Korean government were to issue money indefinitely.

In the case of South Korea, the won is not yet considered to be very safe compared to the dollar, which is classified as a reserve currency, so it has sufficient foreign exchange reserves in case of a dangerous situation such as a financial crisis.
In the case of developing countries, a shortage of the dollar can lead to a serious economic crisis, which was the case in Korea in 1997.

While South Koreans don't pay much attention to the amount of gold held by the central bank, they do pay attention to the country's foreign exchange reserves, which are released monthly.

This may be due to the painful memories of 1997, but just as people used to care about the amount of gold they had, they have shifted their attention to the amount of dollars the government holds.

Perhaps the world is off the gold standard, but the dollar standard has been around since the gold standard, with the dollar as the reserve currency replacing the role of gold.

It is also necessary to think about the mechanisms for maintaining and maintaining the value of Bitcoin.

Unlike government-issued currency, which has a government guarantee, privately issued coins are basically priced by supply and demand, and the demand does not have its own value like gold or silver.

However, if a country such as El Salvador adopts Bitcoin as a means of transaction, it may have value as a currency, but I wonder if Bitcoin, which is highly volatile in price and has weaknesses in terms of payment guarantees, can survive without a means of preserving the value of the dollar or the gold standard, which have historically been subject to fierce competition and debate.

Economic crises caused by currency over-issuance, and exchange rate maintenance policies

The first examples of inflation have to be traced back to ancient Rome. During the reign of Emperor Augustus in Ancient Rome, there was indeed a period of inflation, although it was different from today's concept of inflation.

Inflation during Augustus' reign was caused by a combination of factors, including increased government spending, decreased supply of precious metals used as currency, and increased demand for goods and services, but Augustus also spent a lot of money on war and infrastructure, which put a lot of pressure on the government's finances.

In addition, the supply of gold, silver, and other precious metals used as currency in the Roman Empire was declining, and the expansion of the Roman Empire increased the demand for goods and services, further driving up prices.

The effects of Augustan inflation made it difficult for the poor and working class to make ends meet, leading to social unrest and violent protests.

In response to inflation, Augustus implemented a variety of policies, including price controls and monetary reform, but their effectiveness in stabilizing prices was limited, and inflation continued to be a problem throughout the history of the Roman Empire.

In particular, during the reign of Emperor Nero, he devalued the currency by reducing the amount of silver in each coin and replacing it with cheaper metals such as copper.

This was done to pay for Nero's extravagant spending and wars, but it also contributed to inflation and a decline in the value of Roman currency.

In ancient Rome, coins contained less and less gold, silver, and other precious metals as the emperors wanted to increase the supply of money despite limited reserves of these metals.

People began to spend the coins with the least amount of precious metals in them, i.e., the ones with the lowest real intrinsic value, and keep the ones with the most precious metals. Inherent in this is the risk of inflation and currency devaluation.

For example, suppose a coin containing 10 grams of gold is put into circulation as a $100 gold coin.

Today's gold coin contains 10 grams of gold, but a month from now, the coin will contain 9 grams of gold, and two months from now, it will contain 8 grams of gold.

Nevertheless, when the 10-gram gold coin, the 9-gram gold coin, and the 8-gram gold coin are in circulation, they will be used as $100 gold coins.

There would be no need to use the 10-gram gold coin, which has a higher intrinsic value.
It would make sense to use the gold coin with the least amount of gold and store the gold coin with the most gold.
This is because if a gold coin with 5 grams of gold is later used as a $100 gold coin, a gold coin with 10 grams of gold would theoretically be worth $200.

This monetary behavior resulted in coins with low precious metal content remaining in active circulation and coins with high precious metal content disappearing from the market.
Thomas Gresham, a 16th-century English economist, called this phenomenon "deterioration builds positivity," and it is known as Gresham's Law.

Gresham's law explains that when two forms of money with the same denomination but different intrinsic values are in circulation, the one with the lower intrinsic value tends to drive the one with the higher intrinsic value out of circulation.
From ancient times to modern times, war has been the most common cause of this phenomenon of Gresham's law, whereby deterioration builds up.

Since ancient Rome, wars have been a major cause of inflation, and the relationship between war and inflation has not been broken in modern times, including World Wars I and II and the Russian-Ukrainian War.
There are several ways wars can cause inflation.

First, there is the increased demand for goods and services during wartime, as governments increase procurement of war materials.
Second, wars can disrupt supply chains and trade routes, limiting the availability of goods and services.
This can lead to higher prices because suppliers can pass on greater costs to their goods to compensate for the added risk and expense of transporting goods.
Third, war can lead to a reduced supply of labor and resources. When many able-bodied workers are drafted into the military, there is less labor available to produce goods and services.

In addition, resources such as oil and metals can be diverted for war purposes, limiting their availability for civilian consumption or production, causing resource prices to rise.
Finally, wars can lead to currency devaluation in the countries of the warring

parties. Heavy government spending and borrowing to finance the cost of war dramatically increases the supply of money, which leads to inflation and a decline in the value of money.

From ancient times to the Middle Ages, the inflationary side effects of these wars and the problem of government debt, including government bonds issued to pay for them, have always been a headache for politicians and bureaucrats. Under pressure to solve these problems, government officials and central bankers in medieval Europe were tempted, and even practiced, the unlimited printing of money as a means of financing and solving debt problems.

However, the process of printing money to pay for wars and pay down debt has had a number of side effects across the economy, including extreme inflation, devaluation of the currency, and a decline in trust in the government. These side effects often lead to financial market crashes and economic crises.

Under the gold standard, the finite reserves of gold acted as a constraint on the circulation of money to some extent, but since 1971, when the gold standard was abandoned, this constraint has been removed, and it is easy to see how a policy of monetary excess, implemented to avert a short-term crisis, can lead to a larger crisis, despite the need for careful management by government officials. Along with the quantity of money, policymakers are tempted to manipulate the exchange rate.

Depending on the supply of money, as the supply decreases, the exchange rate increases (appreciation) and as the supply increases, the exchange rate decreases (depreciation), so they are tempted to manipulate the exchange rate by controlling the amount of money in their currency.

Countries typically implement policies to appreciate their currencies (high exchange rates) for the following reasons
Increase purchasing power

A high exchange rate means that imports are cheaper, giving consumers more purchasing power.
This can be especially important for countries that are highly dependent on imports for certain commodities, such as oil.

Controlling inflation
By making imported goods cheaper and reducing the cost of production inputs, such as imported raw materials, it can help curb inflation.

This can be especially important in countries suffering from inflation.

Reduced debt
If you have a lot of foreign currency-denominated debt or foreign-sourced funds, you will most likely be repaying them in local currency terms, so a higher exchange rate will have the effect of reducing the amount you have to repay.

Increased foreign investment
When the exchange rate is high, foreign capital inflows increase and foreign investment increases, but when the exchange rate falls, there is a sharp outflow of foreign capital.
However, it can make exports more expensive, making them less competitive in the global market and reducing exports, and it can cause serious foreign currency outflows if the country tries to keep the exchange rate too high compared to its intrinsic value.
Conversely, there are cases where the goal is to improve the balance of payments by maintaining a low exchange rate policy, i.e., a devaluation that favors export competitiveness.

In particular, countries that have pegged their exchange rates to the U.S. dollar to combat excessive inflation have been able to stabilize their economies by eliminating immediate exchange rate fluctuations.

However, when the value of the dollar changed in response to U.S. monetary policy, it was not accompanied by a change in the intrinsic value of the local currency, which often diverged from the true intrinsic value.

As the exchange rate did not reflect the true intrinsic value of the currency, a black market was created where the currency was traded at a different price from the official exchange rate, and it was often targeted by speculators, leading to economic crises.

If the U.S. interest rate hike increases the value of the dollar, or if the U.S. Fed's quantitative easing increases the money supply and depreciates the dollar, or if the fear of the coronavirus pandemic creates a preference for the dollar, the value of the local currency should fluctuate accordingly.

In addition, the exchange rate of the local currency should fluctuate naturally due to the inflow and outflow of dollars due to trade deficits or surpluses through trade with the U.S. However, there are many cases where a rigid exchange rate system has caused a gap between the intrinsic value of the local currency and the official exchange rate, resulting in economic crises such as foreign exchange crises.

In order to maintain a fixed exchange rate, interest rates or the amount of money must be adjusted, and the effects of the government's delicate monetary policy and market intervention may not work as desired.
This is a weakness that can be exploited by speculators, especially if liquidity is not readily available against the dollar.

A close example is the high exchange rate policy implemented by the Kim Young-sam government prior to South Korea's IMF bailout.
South Korea needed to achieve a per capita income of $20,000 to join the Organization for Economic Cooperation and Development (OECD), which was pushing to be recognized as a developed country at the time, and given the process of calculating per capita income in dollars, it was advantageous to maintain an appreciating exchange rate.

The exchange rate of the won against the dollar, which was over 800 won when President Kim Young-sam took office, fell to the mid-700s in the aftermath of the high exchange rate policy, appreciating to nearly 100 won. In the process, the price of South Korean exports rose, widening the trade deficit, which was one of the factors that led to the depletion of foreign reserves.

The aftermath of the depletion of foreign exchange reserves, coupled with the currency crisis in Southeast Asia, including Thailand, led to the unprecedented situation of applying for an IMF bailout.

In addition, crises caused by excessive currency overhang and the failure of artificial exchange rate maintenance policies can lead to a sudden loss of confidence in a country's currency, resulting in a sharp devaluation and subsequent economic crisis.
Here are some examples of financial crises caused by excessive currency.

Asian Financial Crisis (1997-1998)
Thailand's economic crisis in the late 1990s was caused in large part by the country's decision to peg its currency, the baht, to the U.S. dollar. The peg fixed the exchange rate between the baht and the dollar, which meant that the Bank of Thailand had to maintain the exchange rate by buying and selling dollars on the foreign exchange market.

The peg led to Thailand's economic crisis for the following reasons
Overvalued currency

The fixed exchange rate caused the baht to become overvalued against other currencies, including those of Thailand's trading partners.

This made Thai exports more expensive and less competitive in the global market, leading to a decline in exports and a widening trade deficit.

Foreign speculative capital inflows
The fixed exchange rate has made Thailand an attractive destination for foreign investors as it provides a stable investment environment and guarantees a fixed exchange rate. As a result, there has been a large influx of foreign capital that is more speculative than productive.

Rising external debt
The influx of foreign capital led to a sharp increase in Thailand's external debt, which made the country vulnerable to sudden changes in investor sentiment.

When investor confidence began to decline, many foreign investors began to pull their money out of Thailand, and the country's financial system was threatened by a sudden capital outflow.

In July 1997, the Thai government was forced to devalue the baht in response to speculative attacks on the currency. Following this crisis, the financial crisis spread throughout Southeast and East Asia as Indonesia, Malaysia, the Philippines, South Korea, and Hong Kong began to lose confidence in foreign investors.

Thailand's peg to the U.S. dollar contributed to the country's economic crisis by attracting speculative capital inflows that overvalued the baht and increased external debt.

When investor sentiment turned negative, Thailand was unable to maintain a fixed exchange rate, triggering a financial crisis that spread across the region.

Mexican Peso Crisis (1994-1995)
The Mexican government maintained an overvalued exchange rate against the peso for many years to attract foreign investment, control inflation, and protect domestic industries.

However, maintaining an overvalued exchange rate was not sustainable in the long run and contributed to the economic imbalances that eventually led to the peso crisis.

Mexico's peso crisis was a financial crisis that began in December 1994 and lasted until early 1995.

In December 1994, the Mexican government announced a 15% devaluation of the peso to boost exports and reduce the current account deficit. However, the devaluation caused the peso to plummet as foreign investors sought to sell their Mexican assets.

The Mexican government raised interest rates by up to 80% to stabilize the currency, but this exacerbated the recession and led to bankruptcies and job losses.

The Mexican government turned to the United States and the International Monetary Fund (IMF) for assistance to resolve the crisis, eventually securing a $50 billion bailout.

The crisis had a significant impact on the Mexican economy, with gross domestic product (GDP) falling by about 6% in 1995, and led to reforms to address the underlying economic imbalances that led to the crisis.

Mexico maintained a high exchange rate policy during the peso crisis because it was seen as a way to attract foreign investment, control inflation, and protect domestic industries.

However, this policy created unsustainable economic imbalances in the long run and ultimately contributed to the severity of the crisis.

Russian Financial Crisis (1998)

Russia faced an economic crisis in the late 1990s due to its policy of maintaining an undervalued exchange rate. In the early 1990s, the Russian government implemented a policy of maintaining a devalued exchange rate against its national currency, the ruble, to boost exports and stimulate economic growth.

However, this policy had several negative consequences and eventually led to the crisis.

Inflation

The low exchange rate made imports more expensive, which led to higher inflation in Russia.

This made it more difficult for the government to control inflation through monetary policy because the low exchange rate was putting upward pressure on prices.

Capital outflows

The low exchange rate also made it more attractive for Russian citizens and businesses to hold their wealth in foreign currencies because the ruble was losing value against other currencies.

This has led to a significant amount of capital flight from Russia, which has depleted the country's foreign exchange reserves and made it difficult to obtain foreign currency for imports.

Debt repayment
The low exchange rate policy also made it more difficult for Russia to repay its foreign currency-denominated external debt. As the ruble lost value, the amount of rubles needed to service the debt increased, straining the country's finances.

In August 1998, these policy failures, coupled with a decline in state revenues due to the fall in oil prices at the time, led the Russian government to devalue the ruble and declare a moratorium on some external debt defaults, triggering a financial crisis that led to a sharp contraction in economic activity and a sharp rise in inflation.

The crisis had significant spillover effects on other countries, as Russia's revenues declined and it was unable to pay its foreign creditors.
Russia's low exchange rate policy contributed to the economic crisis by causing inflation, encouraging capital flight, and making it more difficult to repay foreign debt.

When the government recognized that it could no longer maintain a low exchange rate and declared a moratorium, it triggered a financial crisis that had significant spillover effects on other countries.

German hyperinflation in the 1920s
The hyperinflation caused by an oversupply of money in Germany in the 1920s was one of the most severe cases of hyperinflation in history.
After its defeat in World War I, Germany faced a huge debt burden and had to pay war reparations to the Allies.
To pay off these debts, the German government decided to print a lot of money, which greatly increased the money supply.

At first, the increase in the money supply didn't have much effect on prices. However, as more money became available, people began to realize that the value of the German Mark was rapidly decreasing. This led to a loss of confidence in the currency, which in turn led to a rise in inflation.
Despite the rapidly rising prices, the German government exacerbated the problem by printing more money. By 1923, prices for staples were doubling

every few days, and people had to carry wheelbarrows full of cash just to buy basic goods.

The all-too-famous anecdote of a thief stealing a wheelbarrow full of cash and running off with it, leaving the cash behind and taking the wheelbarrow with him, is often cited when discussing the ravages of inflation. At the time, the German mark was depreciating to the point where it was considered less valuable than a wheelbarrow.

Hyperinflation had a profound effect on German society. People's savings were wiped out and people on fixed incomes, such as pensioners, became poorer.

The middle class was particularly hard hit, as their savings became worthless and they lost economic stability. Some people resorted to bartering goods and services instead of spending money.
Hyperinflation also had political implications, as it reduced trust in the government and contributed to the rise of extremist groups like the Nazi Party.

The hyperinflation caused by German monetary excesses in the 1920s was a devastating event that had a profound impact on German society and contributed to the instability of the post-war period.

Zimbabwean hyperinflation (2008-2009)
The Zimbabwean government printed excessive amounts of money to finance its fiscal deficit, which led to hyperinflation and currency collapse.
Hyperinflation is when a country's inflation rate is so high that the prices of goods and services rise uncontrollably, and the country's currency becomes almost worthless.

Zimbabwe had already experienced hyperinflation in the early 2000s, when prices doubled from daily peaks. Zimbabwe's case is one of the most severe cases of hyperinflation in modern history, starting in the late 1990s and peaking in 2008.

Zimbabwe's hyperinflation was caused by a combination of factors, including
Economic mismanagement
The Zimbabwean government engaged in policies that contributed to the economic collapse, such as seizing land from white farmers without compensation, which disrupted the country's agricultural sector and reduced food production. In addition, government spending exceeded revenues, leading to a huge fiscal deficit and a reliance on money printing to finance government activities.

Currency devaluation
The government also devalued the Zimbabwean dollar in an attempt to make exports more competitive and reduce the country's trade deficit.
However, this devaluation led to a loss of confidence in the currency as people realized that their savings were rapidly losing value.

Political instability
Political instability in Zimbabwe, including the contested 2008 elections and violence against the opposition, contributed to the economic crisis by undermining investor confidence and reducing foreign aid.

As a result of these factors, Zimbabwe's inflation rate began to spiral out of control. In 2007, prices rose an average of 98% per day, and by November 2008, the annualized inflation rate had reached 89,700 trillion% (89,700,000,000,000,000,000%).

Hyperinflation had a devastating effect on the Zimbabwean economy and people. Savings were wiped out, businesses closed, and basic necessities like food and medicine became unaffordable.
The government eventually abandoned the Zimbabwean dollar in 2009 and now uses a combination of foreign currencies.

Zimbabwe's hyperinflation was caused by a combination of economic conditions, reckless spending, currency devaluation, and political instability that led to a loss of confidence in the currency and rapidly rising prices.

Hyperinflation had a devastating impact on the economy and people of Zimbabwe, with many losing their savings and unable to afford basic necessities.

Venezuelan Economic Crisis (2014-present)
The Venezuelan government maintained strict currency controls and printed excessive amounts of money to finance its fiscal deficit, leading to hyperinflation and a collapse in the value of the currency. Venezuela's economic crisis was caused by a combination of factors, one of which was excessive printing.

Venezuela has a long history of government intervention in the economy, including the nationalization of industries and price controls. In the early 2000s, the government under President Hugo Chavez began printing large amounts of currency to fund social programs and government spending. This led to a significant increase in the money supply, which in turn led to inflation.

As inflation continued to rise, the government responded by imposing price controls on goods and services, which led to shortages of basic goods such as food and medicine.
The government also restricted access to foreign currency, which made it difficult for businesses to import goods or pay foreign debt. Venezuela's inflation rate exceeded 2,600% per year in 2017.

Hyperinflation is due to a combination of factors, including the decline in the price of oil, Venezuela's main export, as well as excessive government spending, corruption, mismanagement, and restrictions on currency exchange.
Hyperinflation has led to shortages of basic goods, high unemployment, widespread poverty, and mass migration of people trying to escape the country. Excessive monetary over-expansion and the resulting inflation, combined with other factors, led to Venezuela's economic crisis, which has had a devastating impact on the country and its people.

Inflation, interest rates, and exchange rates

1. Inflation

The price of money, or the value of things, is inversely proportional to the value of money. If you paid $35 for an ounce of gold in 1971, you would have to pay $1,000 to buy it in 1980.

Assuming that the value of gold doesn't change, this means that the value of gold hasn't changed, but the value of the dollar has decreased, so you need to give more dollars to buy an ounce of gold.

If we were to value gold based on the current price of gold, an ounce of gold in 1971 would be worth $35 and in 2023 it would be worth over $2,000, which is an increase of about 57 times in about 50 years. However, if you value the dollar in terms of gold, it has depreciated 57 times.

For example, if you bought a hamburger at a McDonald's restaurant a year ago for $4 and today it costs $8, how much has the dollar depreciated?

The price of the hamburger has doubled, but the value of the dollar has decreased by a factor of two.

In other words, the price of the hamburger has doubled and the value of the dollar has decreased.

This example is based on the extreme assumption that the only item measuring inflation is gold or a hamburger.

The most commonly used measures of real-world inflation are the Consumer Price Index (CPI) and the Producer Price Index (PPI), which are calculated by averaging the prices of goods and services consumed or produced in the real world.

However, the prices of real estate and stocks are typically not included in these measures of inflation.

Because real estate and stocks are considered assets, not goods or services, and because they represent ownership of a physical or financial asset rather than a direct purchase of goods or services, their prices are subject to different market forces than the prices of goods and services.

In addition, the prices of real estate and stocks are generally more volatile than the prices of goods and services.

Therefore, it is common for these assets to be excluded from inflation measurements because their inclusion in the inflation measure would increase the volatility of the inflation rate, which could lead to errors in the inflation measure.

When this inflation occurs, the value of your cash is decreasing day by day, and you are better off spending or investing.

In countries that experienced hyperinflation in South America, it was common for people to spend all of their payday deposits on the same day.
This is because the prices of basic necessities keep rising, and spending today is the cheapest way to buy them.

Will the cash I receive in my paycheck today hold its value a year from now? Assuming an inflation rate of 10%, I can expect my cash to be worth 10% less in a year's time.
What can I do to preserve the value of my cash? If I deposit it in a bank and earn 10% interest, I'm preserving the value of my money today.

And if you earn 15% interest, your real interest rate, minus the rate of inflation, is 5%, so you're getting paid for your savings by giving up current consumption. Interest is the reward for sacrificing current consumption of money.
When you invest or save, you are sacrificing and giving up current consumption for future consumption, and the reward for that sacrifice and giving up is interest.

If we assume that the rate of inflation is expected to be 10% and the interest rate on bank deposits or the current issue rate of U.S. Treasury bonds is 20%, people will deposit their money in banks or invest in Treasury bonds.
This increase in interest rates will suck the currency out of the market and into the bank. As the supply of money in circulation decreases, the value of money increases and inflation decreases. This is because an increase in interest rates means an increase in the value of money.

Inflation basically means that the value of money is decreasing. So, in theory, the currency of a country with relatively high inflation should be devalued more than the currency of a country with lower inflation.
The currency of a country with severe inflation, such as a country like Zimbabwe with a trillion-dollar bill, will depreciate faster and more than the currency of a country with relatively low inflation, such as Japan.

And in order to defend the value of a declining currency, the interest that people receive for depositing their money in a bank needs to be increased so that they don't lose money on it.
If the interest rate is lower than inflation, the real interest rate is negative, so the interest rate must be at least as high as the rate of inflation in order for the bank to attract deposits.

2. Interest rates

Monetary tightening, by siphoning money out of the market and into the bank, reduces the demand for goods and thus keeps prices in check, so it is inevitable that interest rates will continue to rise as prices rise.

In addition, if the interest rate is low compared to other countries, the value of the local currency will decrease due to the outflow of funds to overseas countries with higher interest rates, so for the stability of the exchange rate, it is necessary to watch the interest rate situation of other countries and adjust to the interest rate changes.

If the interest rate in the U.S. is higher than the interest rate in Korea, foreigners who have invested in Korea will try to sell the won (increasing the supply of the won, decreasing the value of the won) and buy dollars (increasing the demand for dollars, increasing the value of the dollar) and leave for the U.S., so the value of the won will decrease and the value of the dollar will increase.
If the exchange rate stabilizes due to an increase in interest rates, inflation will be controlled by stabilizing import prices.

However, there are limits to using higher interest rates to control inflation. Raising interest rates, which cannot be done arbitrarily, reduces the supply of money and increases the interest burden on households and businesses with debt, causing the economy to stagnate.

In addition, in the modern era of financial institutions, there are more side effects caused by high interest rates than low interest rates. The S&L crisis in the United States and the savings bank crisis in South Korea are typical examples of financial institution failures that occurred during periods of rising interest rates.

Savings banks in the second tier, which compete with commercial banks in the first tier, have to offer higher interest rates than commercial banks to attract deposits, and the problem is that they have to earn higher returns to survive.

As the saying goes, high risk, high reward, and in order to generate high returns, they must take on high risk. They have been a major source of bankruptcies during rising interest rates, as high-risk investments such as commercial real estate, junk bonds, MBS, and real estate PFs have led to massive losses.

In particular, rising interest rates are a red flag because real estate prices often plummet during periods of rising interest rates due to economic downturns and higher leverage costs.

In addition, there is an inverse relationship between rising interest rates and falling bond prices. To see this, let's look at the trading of bonds that have the same terms other than interest rates, such as credit ratings.

Suppose a bond issued yesterday has a surface interest rate of 5%, and the face value of the bond in the market is $10.

The market price of the bond issued yesterday would have been the par value of $10.

Since the market interest rate yesterday was 5%, and the bonds issued at a 5% surface rate will be digested by institutions, the current surface rate represents the current market interest rate level.

However, if a bond is issued today with a 6% coupon, we can say that the market rate has increased to 6%, and in this situation, what will be the price of a bond issued yesterday with a 5% coupon? Today, the bond with a 6% coupon will trade at $10.

If a bond with a 6% coupon is trading at $10, wouldn't a bond with a worse coupon of 5% have to be priced lower than yesterday's $10 to sell?

Conversely, if a bond issued today with a 4% coupon rate has fallen to 4% in the market, and is trading at $10 today, wouldn't a bond with a better coupon rate of 5% be able to sell for more than yesterday's $10?

In the bond market, this is why the price of bonds goes down when the market interest rate goes up, and the price of bonds goes up when the interest rate goes down.

The reason why the bond market is important is that unlike stocks, even if you lose money on the market price of a bond, if you hold it to maturity, you will receive your principal and interest as long as the issuer does not go bankrupt, so it is used by many institutional investors as a safe investment vehicle.

However, the downside is that if you don't hold it to maturity, you may have liquidity problems and may even lose money, which is what happened with the bankruptcy of the Bank of Silicon Valley in March 2023.

The large amount of money released to combat the pandemic and the retaliatory spending after the pandemic led to inflation, which was intensified by Russia's invasion of Ukraine, which pushed up energy prices, prompting the U.S. Federal Reserve to raise interest rates steeply through the Federal Open Market Committee (FOMC).

Silicon Valley Bank, which invested its deposits in safe assets such as U.S. Treasury bonds for a long period of time during the low interest rate situation, was a bank with a very high proportion of U.S. Treasury bonds.

When the bank was asked to pay short-term deposits, it had to sell long-term Treasury bonds to pay short-term deposits, but the price of Treasury bonds plummeted due to the increase in interest rates, and the bank was forced to sell the bonds at a loss.

The losses on the sale of these bonds were then reflected in the financial statements, resulting in a deficit.
When the bank's losses on the bonds were publicized through various media, nervous depositors withdrew their deposits, triggering a bank run, and Silicon Valley Bank was unable to overcome the liquidity shortage and went bankrupt.
The risk of maturity mismatch between short-term financing and long-term funding had already been demonstrated in the financing and management behavior of Korean financial conglomerates during the Korean financial crisis.

However, it is pointed out that although it was the worst situation where several risk factors occurred at once, such as the bankruptcy of the debtor, the problem of hedging the exchange rate risk due to procurement and operation of different foreign currencies, and the suspension of the extension of short-term funds, it was necessary to prepare countermeasures for risk management and internal checks such as stress tests.
Banks are basically in the business of raising short-term funds to lend long-term funds and enjoy a margin of safety.

The expansion of margins specifically enhances profitability if short-term interest rates decline while central banks lower long-term interest rates with a lag.
Long-term interest rates will be impacted over time by the decline in short-term rates, and when long-term interest rates fall, so will the associated real estate mortgage rates.

The liquidity released in the market flows into the real estate market, creating a real estate bubble with lower leverage, and banks increase their real estate lending.
Conversely, if a central bank raises its benchmark interest rate, the time lag may cause the long-term rate to stay the same, reversing the relationship between long-term and short-term interest rates.

Commercial banks have to pay higher interest rates to their short-term deposit customers, while their long-term loan customers' rates do not increase, creating a reverse margin.

Eventually, banks will have no choice but to increase their long-term interest rates, which will push up long-term interest rates, and this inversion of short-term and long-term interest rates can be dangerous.

It is only a matter of time before the real estate bubble bursts due to the increase in long-term interest rates while short-term interest rates remain at the same level. Also, it is common for long-term interest rates to be higher than short-term interest rates due to inflation, asset appreciation, and compensation for liquidity premiums.

However, when this is reversed, it is seen as a warning sign of a recession, as it suggests that investors have a negative long-term economic outlook.

If the central bank sets a target for inflation, and the central bank raises interest rates to fight inflation, the real estate market may face a bubble bursting situation as leverage costs rise.

And the bursting of real estate bubbles, which in turn cause the failure of banks as a source of financing, leading to financial crises, has been a typical form of economic crisis since the 20th century.

These crises, caused by the expansion and contraction of currencies, have been cyclical, like the cycles of the business cycle, and have led to the failure of many financial institutions.

The risk of a mismatch in the maturity structure of funds is often inherent in the business model of the receiving financial institution. Therefore, the establishment and review of management techniques such as Asset & Liability Management (ALM) to prepare for such risks is an essential survival strategy for recipient financial institutions.

Although the modern financial system is a complex structure with many derivatives, it is still a system that deals with the essential product of money, and changes in interest rates, which can be seen as the use price for money, have many effects on financial markets such as inflation, the stock market, and the bond market.

In particular, interest rate movements in the bond market provide useful information about the flow of money. Government bonds traded in the secondary market have interest rates that are inversely proportional to their credit rating by a rating agency.

If a country has an excellent credit rating, such as the United States or Japan, it can be issued at a low interest rate, while the interest rate of government bonds of less developed or developing countries is relatively high.

Public funds and pension funds in countries that have increased their foreign exchange reserves due to the accumulation of trade surpluses or rising prices of resources tend to favor government bonds or bonds with high credit ratings to safely manage foreign currency.

In particular, the sovereign bond market is sensitive to economic crises, and an increase in the interest rate of a country's sovereign bonds is accompanied by an increase in risk indices such as the country's credit default swap (CDS), which is a red flag that investors believe that the country's economic prospects are negative.

Therefore, during a crisis, you can get a sense of the true value of a country's economy by looking at which countries' sovereign bond rates stay the same and which ones rise.

In times of economic crisis, the interest rates on government bonds issued by countries such as the United States, Japan, and Germany tend to decrease, and the interest rates on government bonds of other countries that are considered safe decrease.

Conversely, interest rates on sovereign bonds that are considered risky tend to rise.

As the crisis deepens, U.S. Treasury yields will fall further, and yields on Treasuries of developed countries with lower credit ratings than the U.S. will rise slightly.

Therefore, a country with sufficient foreign exchange reserves, a clean credit rating, and a steady trade surplus is unlikely to experience a sharp rise in CDS or a sharp rise in sovereign interest rates during an economic crisis.

If investors analyze the country's various economic indicators and determine that there is no cause for concern, the market is unlikely to take any action to withdraw funds. In general, inflation, interest rates, and exchange rates interact with each other and self-correct through international trade.

3. Exchange rates

Looking back at the situation in South Korea before and after the 1997 Asian financial crisis, we can see the role that self-correction played.

When the 1995 reverse plaza agreement devalued the yen against the dollar, making Japanese exports more competitive in overseas markets such as the U.S.

market, Korean exports competing with Japanese goods in overseas markets became relatively more expensive, widening Korea's trade deficit.

This meant an outflow of foreign currency, which was accompanied by an appreciation of the dollar in the foreign exchange market and a depreciation of the won in the foreign exchange market.
The logic of self-correction in international trade is that the price of South Korea's exports decreases, leading to an increase in exports, and the price of imports increases, leading to a decrease in imports, leading to a convergence of the trade deficit to balance.

However, artificially preventing prices from rising and prices from falling can have adverse effects, as seen in the case of price and quantity controls that led to shortages of items such as masks during the coronavirus pandemic, and in the case of Robespierre's milk price controls during the French Revolution, which caused milk and feed prices to skyrocket.

At the time, South Korea's exchange rate system was based on a market rate.
The exchange rate was set by a volume-weighted average of the quotations of foreign exchange banks on the same day, but it was a rigid system that limited the amount of daily fluctuation up or down.
The rate had been adjusted to fluctuate within 0.4% in March 1990, 1.5% in November 1994, and 2.25% in December 1995.

However, when the exchange rate was capped at 2.25% in early 1997, it was unable to keep up with the demand for dollars to go out of the country as Koreans sensed a crisis in the economy and sold the won to buy dollars.
Currently, the daily fluctuation of the Korean stock market is capped at 30% for the upside and 30% for the downside. However, stocks with high or low intrinsic value can be at the upper or lower limit for days at a time.

This is because the artificial price control extends the time to reach the true value.
However, the problem arises with volume. People who think it's going to go up won't sell at this price, and people who think it's going to go down won't buy at this price, so there's very little trading going on. Eventually, only after a significant price correction does the volume start to explode.

This is what happened in 1997, and it made it difficult to get dollars.
On November 20, 1997, the daily fluctuation of the exchange rate was increased to 10%, but the rate of depreciation and fluctuation of the won was much higher than that. Eventually, on December 16, 1997, the daily fluctuation limit was

completely abolished and a free floating exchange rate system was introduced.

The exchange rate of the won to the dollar fluctuated above 2,000 won, but it stabilized over time, and Korea became a trade surplus country in 1998, as the devaluation of the won made its exports more competitive.
The introduction of a free-floating exchange rate system allowed self-correction to work properly.

The fixed or managed floating exchange rate system is considered a type of artificial price control policy due to the rigidity of the exchange rate fluctuation, and it caused the self-correction in international trade to fail.
In addition to exchange rates, there are also cases of active market intervention by governments to reverse the self-correcting effects of international trade.

The case of trade between the United States and China is an example of government intervention to prevent this self-correction.
The United States has a growing trade deficit with China, and China has a growing trade surplus with the United States.
In theory, the U.S. should have a weaker dollar through dollar outflows, and China should have a stronger yuan through a self-correcting trade balance, but the trade imbalance between the two countries still persists.

In a normal situation, the U.S. would have an excessive trade deficit, causing the dollar to weaken and the price of imported goods to rise, resulting in inflation.
Then, to control inflation, interest rates are raised, creating a sequence of weak dollar, high prices, and high interest rates, but in the case of the US, this self-correcting system is not working.

From the U.S. perspective, the trade deficit is offset by a capital account surplus, which prevents the usual inflation and high interest rates.
From China's perspective, increased exports to the U.S. could lead to a depreciation of the dollar and an appreciation of the yuan, China's domestic currency.

In such a situation, China's central bank could take a policy of expanding the amount of currency in the market by printing yuan to buy dollars coming into the country and then exchanging them for dollars, a policy known as a monetization policy.

If the Chinese central bank issues yuan to buy dollars through the trade surplus with the United States, the supply of yuan in the market will increase, and the process of foreign currency supply leading to domestic currency expansion is said to be like laying an egg.

However, if a lot of money is released in the market through the policy, it has the side effect of causing domestic inflation.

Therefore, to prevent inflation, the central bank can issue government bonds, such as currency stability bonds, to capture the RMB released from the market, and the increase in currency volume through trade surpluses can absorb the sale of government bonds.

This is the opposite of a sterilization policy, which can be described in various ways, including sterilization, sterilization, and sterility.

To summarize, the Chinese central bank purchases dollars earned in the U.S. by issuing yuan, and the yuan that is released into the market is repurchased by issuing government bonds to protect against inflation.

The yuan is then used to buy U.S. Treasuries, which in turn are used to protect the dollar from depreciation.

The larger the cumulative trade surplus with the United States, the greater the amount of government bonds the Chinese government issues to implement these policies.

This increased the interest burden that the Chinese government had to pay on the bonds, which increased the fiscal burden on the Chinese government.

As in the case of Japan, more government bond issuance leads to a decrease in the price of government bonds and an increase in government bond interest rates, which is why China has implemented an interest rate control policy.

The deposit rate is controlled at 1.5%-2%, and the lending rate is controlled at 4-5%.

While companies are able to borrow at low interest rates given the economic growth and inflation rates, making their exports more cost-competitive, savers are deprived of investment opportunities that could have yielded higher returns.

The government sells low-interest Chinese government bonds to these sacrificing depositors, and controls interest rates so that the interest burden on Chinese government bonds does not increase.

Through these policies, China has been able to adequately defend its exchange rate and inflation, keep interest rates low, and ease its fiscal deficit burden.

From China's perspective, the U.S. is their largest consumer of goods, and as a reserve currency, they would like to maintain the status quo because it is the largest issuer of U.S. Treasury securities.

This relationship between China and the United States is not typical. It is only possible because of special circumstances, such as the US's status as a major power and China's managed economy.

Rather, something like the trade imbalance between Greece and Germany is more typical.

Prior to its financial crisis in 2009, Greece had been accumulating an annual trade deficit with Germany, a manufacturing powerhouse in the Eurozone.

With few competitive industries other than shipping and tourism, Greece was forced to import more from Germany, a global manufacturing powerhouse, after the country's currency was unified under the euro.

The creation of a single currency, the euro, dramatically reduced the transaction costs of trade between countries in the eurozone. This meant that the volume of trade between countries within the eurozone expanded.

While the currencies of the top countries in the eurozone, such as Germany, depreciated as the euro was unified to reflect the average within the eurozone, the currency of the bottom country, Greece, appreciated, so German exports were earning more trade surpluses against the bottom countries in the eurozone.

For Greece, the accumulation of a trade deficit requires the exchange rate to self-correct to reduce the deficit, but the unification of the currency removes this tool.

In the case of the U.S. and China, China's purchases of U.S. Treasuries were correcting the imbalance by allowing the capital account to adjust the trade deficit.

In the case of Greece, it was doing something similar. The outflow of euros from the trade imbalance was compensated for by loans and investments in Greece by foreign banks in the eurozone.

As the trade imbalance grew, Greece's national debt grew, and Greek sovereign debt was not as popular as U.S. Treasuries, so it had to pay higher interest rates, and as a reserve currency, it was not in a position to print money indefinitely.

When the global financial crisis erupted from the United States in 2008 and the world sought safe haven assets, Greece was forced to issue government bonds at higher interest rates to pay off its growing national debt, which the government could not afford and declared a moratorium.

The global economic crisis has proven that when safe-haven assets are favored, the debt of risky countries like Greece will have to pay higher and higher interest rates, and events like the moratorium are more likely to occur.

As global investors tend to seek safe-haven assets with good liquidity whenever there is a crisis, interest rates on risky assets are bound to go higher.

During the recent crisis caused by the bankruptcy of financial institutions in the U.S. and Europe, the Korean stock market fell as foreign investors sold their shares.

However, this was not caused by a negative view of the Korean economy as in the past, but rather by the desire to be the first to sell and cash out of liquid Korean stocks.

To determine whether the exodus of foreign investors is temporary or not, we can look at the government bond market.

If they have a negative view of the Korean economy, they will probably sell Korean government bonds in the government bond market, and if not, they will buy them in a crisis.

In the case of selling Korean government bonds, the price of government bonds would plummet, as happened during the Asian financial crisis, and interest rates would have to rise because new government bonds would have to be issued at higher rates.

However, if the demand from foreign investors to hold Korean government bonds as a safe haven asset increases, the price of government bonds will increase and the interest rate on government bonds will decrease, so the interest rate on government bonds during a crisis can be used to understand how foreign investors view a country's economy.

Even as interest rates are rising in other competitor countries, interest rates in Korea have remained low except for internal issues, so foreign investors' views of the Korean economy are not yet negative.

Quantitative Easing and Modern Monetary Theory (MMT)

1. Overview

In modern countries, the government has a pre-determined and approved national budget and uses the money for social and indirect capital expenditures, welfare, defense, etc. to supply funds to the private sector and stimulate private demand, which is called fiscal policy.

In addition, monetary policy is a policy that affects private demand indirectly by adjusting the benchmark interest rate, buying or selling government bonds in the secondary market, or by adjusting the rediscount rate for money transactions with financial institutions or the percentage of reserves that financial institutions deposit with the central bank.

Those who are more advocates of the effectiveness of monetary policy in this direction of government policy favor the use of monetary policy using interest rate policy, including quantitative easing. On the other hand, economists who advocate Modern Monetary Theory (MMT) argue that the government should be able to use its fiscal power to directly influence the economy, and that fiscal policy is a better tool than monetary policy.

Unlike monetarists who advocate for balanced budgets, advocates of fiscal policy through modern monetary theory argue that deficits are inevitable and that when government finances are excessive, the ticketing power can be used to pay down debt.

In the past, when the real economy was large and the financial system was underdeveloped, the utilization rate and effectiveness of fiscal policy were high, but as the financial system has become more sophisticated and large, the spillover effects of monetary policy have become increasingly large.

In particular, as globalization and the relaxation of financial regulations such as foreign exchange liberalization have allowed capital to move freely across countries, monetary policy is closely related to exchange rate fluctuations and even affects the regulation of foreign exchange.

As the use of leverage has become more common, access to credit and the influence of interest rate policy on asset markets such as real estate and stocks has also increased.

It is a testament to the financial system's influence on the real economy that it is often used to address inflation, an imbalance of prices in the real economy, by raising interest rates.

In the past, downturns or failures in the real economy often triggered crises in financial markets, but in the modern era, crises in the real economy are often triggered by changes in monetary policy, demonstrating the growing dependence of the real economy on the financial system.

This is because the financing of the real economy is increasingly dependent on the financial markets, and as leveraged financing of the real economy becomes more common, a collapse in the real economy can occur if the increase in the cost of leverage is larger and faster than the increase in the price of real assets, which in turn contributes to the collapse of the financial markets.

For this reason, business cycles have been relatively long in the past when government intervention in markets was not active.

However, in the modern era, when government intervention in the market through monetary policy has become commonplace, business cycles are becoming shorter.

In addition to interest rate policy, open market manipulation is a common policy used by central banks to control the amount of money by buying and selling government bonds in the secondary market.

Since financial institutions, including banks, are the main traders in the secondary market for government securities, open market operations affect the amount of money in the private sector by adjusting the money supply of financial institutions.

In contrast, economists who advocate Modern Monetary Theory (MMT) argue that central banks should directly intervene in the primary market.

Critics of MMT argue that issuing government bonds under MMT leads to an increase in the supply of government bonds, a decrease in the price of government bonds, and an increase in government bond yields, or interest rates.

This increase in interest rates has been used as a major argument against MMT because it offsets the effectiveness of fiscal policy to stimulate a depressed economy, and is cited as an example of this phenomenon in the case of Japan's expansionary fiscal policy after the bursting of the bubble, which led to a decline in the real estate market and the failure of financial institutions.

In response to this rebuttal, MMT advocates argue that governments should receive money issued by the central bank through its issuance power directly from the issue market, rather than from the secondary market, to carry out their planned budget.

This way, they argue, when the government issues government bonds, the central bank directly underwrites them in full, shortening the issuance process and speeding up the time it takes for the currency to impact the private sector through faster budget execution.

This direct participation of the central bank in the government bond market is called "monetization of debt".

However, a central bank may prefer to intervene in the government bond market through indirect means, such as open market operations or quantitative easing, rather than providing funds to the government by directly purchasing government bonds for the following reasons.
First, a government's direct dealings with the central bank in the sovereign debt market may raise concerns about the central bank's independence and create inflationary pressures in the real economy.

On the other hand, we believe that indirect intervention methods can be used to influence interest rates and provide liquidity to the financial system without creating the same risks.
Second, it may be seen by financial markets as a sign of fiscal dominance, where the government controls monetary policy to meet fiscal needs, which may undermine the credibility and independence of the central bank, which is important for maintaining price stability and financial stability.

Third, it can be seen as a short-term solution to fiscal problems, leaving much room for abuse by governments.
For these reasons, it is common for central banks to trade sovereign debt in the secondary market, not the primary market.

The main policy instrumental difference between QE and MMT is whether these central banks purchase government bonds in the secondary or primary market. While contemporary monetary theory is divided on QE and MMT, policies such as MMT are considered viable only for countries like the United States and Japan, which have the status of a reserve currency and can export their currency abroad, as they can minimize the side effects of inflation caused by monetary expansion by creating foreign demand for their currency.

2. The Japanese example of QE and monetization of debt
Both QE and the use of MMT were pioneered by Japan, and former US Federal Reserve Chairman Bernanke famously studied Japanese economics to guide US QE policy.

The earliest examples of debt monetization can be found in the 1930s at the Bank of Japan.
In the 1930s, Japan was experiencing an economic downturn due to the global Great Depression and the loss of overseas markets for its exports.
To combat this, the Japanese government needed vast amounts of money,

especially in the areas of military expansion and infrastructure development. However, due to the recession and limited domestic savings, the Japanese government had difficulty raising funds through traditional means such as taxation and borrowing.

To overcome these challenges, the Japanese government decided to use direct financing from the Bank of Japan (BOJ), the country's central bank at the time.

Using its printing presses, the BOJ agreed to use the newly created money to buy Japanese government bonds in the open market, effectively monetizing the government's debt. This process is known as "monetization of debt."

At the time, the BOJ's decision to monetize debt was controversial, as it violated the principle of central bank independence and raised concerns about inflationary pressures. However, the government argued that it was necessary to support the economy and protect national security interests.

The practice of monetizing debt continued throughout the 1930s and was a key element in financing Japan's military expansion in the run-up to World War II. After the war, Japan implemented a number of economic reforms to prevent a recurrence of this policy, including the independence of the Bank of Japan and restrictions on the monetization of debt.

After a period of spectacular economic growth, Japan's economy slowed down in 1985 when the Plaza Accord created an artificially strong yen, and the Japanese government, fearing a recession, adopted monetary easing policies, creating a bubble economy.

However, the bubble began to burst as the Japanese government took steps to raise interest rates and limit the use of real estate leverage due to various adverse effects on the bubble.

In the downward spiral, the Japanese government attempted to stimulate the economy through fiscal policy, but the real estate market deteriorated and financial institutions accumulated bad debts.

After the Plaza Accord of 1985, the exchange rate shift to the yen lasted for a decade, but it did not eliminate the U.S. balance of payments imbalance.

The artificial weakening of the yen through the reverse Plaza Agreement in 1995 began as the United States turned to stimulating the Japanese economy, which had fallen into recession after the Great Kobe Earthquake, and improving its capital account through higher interest rates and a stronger dollar.

This helped Japan's economy rebound, but the 1997 Asian currency crisis hit Japanese investors, many of whom had invested overseas, hard, and Japanese financial institutions, which had been suffering from accumulated insolvency, began to fail one after another.

Although the Japanese government realized that financial institutions were failing and took measures to restructure them, it was not enough to prevent the economy from falling back.

To stimulate the economy, the Bank of Japan (BOJ) implemented a series of unconventional monetary policy measures, including quantitative easing (QE). QE is a monetary policy tool in which a central bank buys large amounts of government bonds or other securities in the open market to increase the money supply and stimulate the economy. The goal is to lower interest rates and increase lending, investment, and consumption.

The BOJ's first round of quantitative easing began in 2001, when it purchased government bonds and other securities from banks to increase the money supply. This policy was expanded in 2006, and the BOJ increased its purchases of government bonds to stimulate the economy and prevent deflation.

The policy was effective in increasing liquidity in the financial system, lowering long-term interest rates, and stimulating lending and investment, but its effectiveness was limited by a lack of demand for credit and weakening consumer confidence.

In 2008, the BOJ further expanded its QE program in response to the global financial crisis, increasing purchases of government bonds and other securities and introducing new measures such as purchases of corporate bonds and exchange-traded funds (ETFs).

When the Abe government took office in 2013, it vowed to stimulate Japan's economy by any means necessary, a policy known as Abenomics.

As part of Abenomics, the BOJ implemented a new quantitative easing program known as "Quantitative and Qualitative Monetary Easing" (QQE), which combined massive asset purchases with other measures such as negative interest rates and forward guidance on policy rates.

This was a policy implemented by the Bank of Japan (BOJ) to end deflation and stimulate the economy, and it expanded its purchases to include not only Japanese government bonds but also other assets such as corporate bonds and exchange-traded funds (ETFs) to increase the money supply and spur economic growth.

In the process of quantitative easing, the BOJ increased the size of its bond purchases, starting with a target of 50 trillion yen per year until the inflation rate reached 2%, and then increasing to 80 trillion yen.

This was done to support the government's efforts to achieve its 2% inflation target and stimulate growth through fiscal stimulus.

While the "quantitative and qualitative monetary easing" (QQE) policy succeeded in boosting asset prices and raising inflation expectations, it failed to achieve the inflation target due to external factors such as low oil prices, weak global demand, and a consumption tax hike.

The BOJ purchased a total of JPY636 trillion worth of Japanese government bonds between 2013 and 2021, and these actions increased the BOJ's asset-to-GDP ratio to over 90% by 2020.

The Bank of Japan's public purchases of government bonds have driven up the price of Japanese government bonds, which, contrary to the Japanese government's wishes, has not had a significant effect on the circulation of money in the market, as private investors and commercial banks have purchased government bonds.

Commercial banks in Japan were constrained in their asset management due to negative interest rates on excess reserves, and were forced to purchase Japanese government bonds, a safe asset, due to regulations on the BIS ratio.

However, the demand for government bonds increased due to the purchase of government bonds by individual investors and commercial banks, and the price of government bonds increased, which led to lower interest rates for new government bond issuance.

As a result, the Japanese government was able to maintain its low interest rate stance and reduce the interest burden on government bonds.

The Bank of Japan has also implemented a number of policies to inject money into the market as part of its quantitative easing policy, including the purchase of approximately ¥35 trillion worth of exchange traded funds (ETFs) and ¥1.5 trillion worth of real estate investment trusts (REITs). These policies have contributed to achieving the goal of ending deflation and boosting economic growth.

In September 2016, the Bank of Japan introduced an additional "Yield Curve Control" (YCC) policy to achieve its 2% inflation target, modeled after Operation Twist, a form of quantitative easing implemented in the United States in the 1960s.

With no room for further monetary policy with an already zero interest rate policy, the Bank of Japan introduced a negative interest rate regime, setting the short-term policy rate at -0.1%.

It also set the 10-year government bond rate at 0% and used its yield curve control policy to keep not only short-term interest rates low, but also medium- and long-term interest rates.

The idea was to keep the yield curve for Japanese government bonds (JGBs) stable and to stimulate the economy by controlling long-term interest rates.
This policy was designed to accomplish the following goals.
First, it aimed to provide a stable and predictable interest rate environment to support investment and consumption. By keeping long-term interest rates low, it sought to reduce borrowing costs for households and businesses to stimulate economic activity.
Second, the policy was intended to support the government's efforts to stimulate the economy through fiscal policy. By keeping yields on Japanese government bonds (JGBs) low, the policy aimed to reduce government borrowing costs and help the government overcome its fiscal deficit.
Third, the policy was aimed at achieving the Bank of Japan's inflation target of 2%. By keeping interest rates low, it encouraged borrowing and spending, which could help increase demand and boost inflation.

This policy helped keep long-term interest rates low and stabilize the yield curve, which provided a predictable environment for investors and supported economic activity. It also helped reduce government borrowing costs and supported the government's fiscal stimulus efforts.

Today, Japan still sets upper and lower limits on government bond yields and uses market intervention to adjust government bond rates within a controlled range, just as the government intervenes in the market under a fixed exchange rate regime.
However, the short-term negative interest rates have led to a shortage of JGBs in the market as Japanese commercial banks, facing funding difficulties, prefer to invest in long-term Japanese government bonds.

The persistently low interest rates also weighed on banks' profitability as net interest margins shrank.
Despite the efforts of the Japanese government and the Bank of Japan, the Japanese economy has not been able to achieve its inflation target through internal stimulus, with the exception of external factors such as the post-COVID-19 pandemic recovery, supply chain disruptions, and the invasion of Ukraine.

Despite Japan's strong monetary easing policy, the following factors have contributed to the difficulty in achieving the 2% inflation target.

Japan is one of the world's largest holders of foreign assets and a creditor nation, with yen carry trade liquidation and safe-haven demand for Japanese government bonds returning in times of crisis.

The demand for government bonds has been robust, keeping interest rates low, and the demand for the yen as a safe haven asset has increased with each crisis, keeping the value of the yen high. With the yen's high value, it has been difficult for inflation to rise.

Another major factor is the ongoing deflationary environment that has been in place for more than 20 years. In Japan, a shrinking and aging population has reduced domestic consumption demand and a shrinking labor force, exacerbating deflationary pressures.
Another factor is a lack of confidence in the future prospects of the economy among consumers and businesses.

If people and businesses are hesitant to spend and invest despite low interest rates and abundant liquidity in the financial system, demand for goods and services will be weak, making it difficult to achieve the inflation target.
In addition, the law of diminishing marginal returns may have reduced the effectiveness of monetary policy in stimulating the economy over time.
In other words, the BOJ's aggressive monetary policy may have lost some of its effectiveness in stimulating borrowing, spending, and investment. A prolonged period of low interest rates is also reducing its effectiveness by making people take low interest rates for granted and dulling their sensitivity to rate cuts.

Finally, there are structural challenges in the Japanese economy that cannot be addressed by monetary policy alone. For example, strict labor market regulations, high corporate taxes, and a lack of entrepreneurial dynamism are all factors that can weigh on economic growth and inflation.

3. Operation Twist
In general, the interest rate policy implemented by the central bank serves to provide liquidity to commercial banks by reducing the base rate when liquidity in the market is depleted and insufficient due to financial crisis.
However, since the benchmark rate is a short-term interest rate, it has the effect of improving liquidity by providing short-term liquidity, but the effect on long-term interest rates may take time.

In the case of Korea, the BOK's benchmark interest rate was the call rate until February 2008, but since then, it has been using the 7-day water repurchase agreement (RP) rate as a benchmark interest rate indicator.

Therefore, to adjust the long-term interest rate, the central bank will utilize open market operations to intervene in the secondary market for long-term government or corporate bonds and purchase long-term bonds.

When the central bank purchases long-term bonds in the secondary market, the demand for long-term bonds increases and the supply of long-term bonds decreases, causing the price of long-term bonds to increase, and newly issued long-term bonds can be issued at lower interest rates, causing the yield on long-term bonds, or long-term interest rates, to decrease.

When the central bank cuts interest rates, short-term interest rates decline quickly, but long-term interest rates decline slowly, so when commercial banks use short-term funds for long-term operations, their profitability improves by increasing their deposit margins.

In addition, long-term interest rates are linked to real estate mortgages, which are long-term loans, and affect the real estate market.

During the 2008 global economic crisis, the U.S. Federal Reserve Bank (FRB) used a policy called "Operation Twist" to induce a decline in long-term interest rates along with quantitative easing to stimulate the real estate market.

Operation Twist was a monetary policy tool used by the U.S. Federal Reserve in the 1960s to influence the shape of the yield curve and spur economic growth.

In the early 1960s, the U.S. lowered its benchmark interest rate to stimulate an economy that had been stagnant since the late 1950s, which led to a decline in short-term interest rates. However, due to the ongoing inflation, the market was expecting inflation and the decline in long-term interest rates was slower.

In addition, the U.S. economy in the early 1960s was characterized by two distinct markets: short-term money markets and long-term bond markets.

Banks and other financial institutions traditionally focused on lending in the short-term money market, where interest rates were determined by FRB policy. Interest rates in the long-term bond market were perceived to be outside of the FRB's control.

This resulted in a widening spread between short-term and long-term interest rates, and the FRB believed that high long-term interest rates hindered U.S. economic growth by reducing the demand for loans from individuals and businesses.

It is normal for long-term rates to be higher than short-term rates because of the liquidity premium paid for giving up liquidity and the compensation for inflation.

However, long-term interest rates are associated with long-term loans, such as real estate-related loans and corporate facility funding, and lowering long-term interest rates has had the effect of stimulating the real estate economy and promoting corporate capital investment.

To this end, the FRB has adopted a strategy of selling short-term Treasury securities in the secondary market and using the proceeds to purchase long-term Treasury securities, known as Operation Twist.

Selling short-term Treasuries causes the price of short-term Treasuries to fall and the short-term interest rate, the yield on short-term Treasuries, to rise.

For example, if you buy a 6-month Treasury bond with a $10,000 principal amount and a 6% coupon rate, the amount you will receive in 6 months is $10,300, assuming no taxes or other costs.

If this bond was selling for $10,000 yesterday and is selling for $9,500 today due to the FRB's market intervention, the yield on the $10,300 bond in six months will be more than 6%, so the decline in the bond price will cause the interest rate to rise.

By the same logic, when the FRB intervenes in the secondary market to purchase long-term Treasury securities, it increases the demand for long-term Treasury securities, which increases the price of long-term Treasury securities, which decreases the yield on long-term Treasury securities, which decreases long-term interest rates.

Rising short-term rates and falling long-term rates have the effect of narrowing the spread, the difference between short-term and long-term rates, which has the effect of flattening the short- and long-term yield curves.

In fact, in 1961, the spread between the 3-month and 10-year Treasury yields was about 2.5%, but by the end of 1962, after Operation Twist, the spread had narrowed to about 1%.

The impact of Operation Twist on the economy was mixed. On the one hand, the drop in long-term interest rates helped spur economic growth by encouraging borrowing and investment. On the other hand, the policy also had unintended consequences, such as the increase in inflation that occurred in the mid-1960s.

Operation Twist was an important innovation in monetary policy because it demonstrated the FRB's ability to influence long-term interest rates through open market operations.

The U.S. FRB had implemented this strategy twice before in the 1960s.

The first was in 1961, when the U.S. economy was growing slowly and unemployment was high, and the FRB sold $1 billion in short-term Treasury securities and used the proceeds to buy long-term Treasury bills and bonds, resulting in a 0.15% reduction in long-term interest rates.

The second time this strategy was used was in 1965. The FRB sold $4 billion in short-term Treasury securities and used the proceeds to buy long-term Treasury securities.

This resulted in a 0.4% cut in long-term interest rates and was successful in stimulating economic growth and lowering unemployment during a period of economic downturn.

After two rounds of quantitative easing in the wake of the 2008 global financial crisis, the FRB reintroduced Operation Twist as a tool to lower long-term interest rates and spur economic growth, despite the need for additional quantitative easing and facing opposition from Congress due to inflation fears.

The global financial crisis triggered by subprime mortgages had led to a downturn in the real estate market, and the FRB hoped that by lowering long-term interest rates, it would reduce the cost of leverage in the real estate market, which was tied to long-term interest rates.

The FRB first announced the reintroduction of its Operation Twist strategy in September 2011, pledging to purchase $400 billion of long-term Treasury securities over the next nine months while selling an equal amount of short-term Treasury securities.

The FRB's long-term Treasury purchases were targeted at U.S. Treasury securities with maturities between six and 30 years.

The Federal Reserve made large purchases of long-term U.S. Treasury bonds and mortgage-backed securities to put downward pressure on long-term interest rates.

By the time the program ended in December 2012, the Fed had purchased $667 billion in U.S. Treasuries, and the interest rate on the 10-year Treasury note had fallen from 2.00% to 1.70%.

These purchases helped lower mortgage rates and other long-term borrowing costs, which supported household spending and business investment activity.

In 2013, the Abe administration came to power in Japan and implemented the so-called Abenomics policy, which aimed to stimulate the economy by achieving an inflation target of at least 2% and revitalizing the economy by any means necessary.

The Bank of Japan (BOJ), Japan's central bank, announced Operation Twist, a form of quantitative easing implemented in the U.S., as a policy called "Yield Curve Control" (YCC).

Japan's Yield Curve Control (YCC) policy, introduced by the Bank of Japan (BOJ) in 2016, was influenced by the Operation Twist strategy.

The YCC policy aimed to control the yield curve by setting a target for the 10-year Japanese government bond (JGB) yield at around 0%, and the BOJ bought or sold JGBs to keep the 10-year JGB yield close to the target level.

While there are similarities between Japan's YCC policy and the Operation Twist strategy used by the U.S. Federal Reserve in the 1960s, there are also important differences in the specific goals, targets, and implementation of the two policies.

While Operation Twist is a strategy of selling short-term bonds and buying long-term bonds, a YCC policy involves setting a yield target for a particular bond and buying or selling bonds to meet that target.

Also, while Operation Twist is a short-term policy response to specific economic conditions, the YCC policy is a long-term policy that has been in place since 2016 and is aimed at achieving the Bank of Japan's 2% inflation rate.

4. Quantitative Easing (QE)

Quantitative easing (QE) is an unconventional monetary policy tool used by central banks to stimulate the economy when traditional policy tools such as interest rate adjustments have lost their effectiveness.

It was first used by the Bank of Japan in the early 2000s and was widely used during the global financial crisis of 2008-09.

Definition

QE is the process by which a central bank injects liquidity into an economy by purchasing assets, typically government bonds, from banks and other financial institutions in the secondary market.

The process aims to increase the supply of money in circulation, making it easier for businesses and individuals to borrow and spend, spurring economic growth and increasing inflation.

How QE works and its effects

The QE process generally involves three main steps.

First, the central bank announces its intention to purchase assets, signaling its willingness to inject liquidity into the market.

Second, the central bank purchases assets, typically government bonds, from banks and other financial institutions to increase the money supply.

Third, banks and financial institutions use the cash they receive from the central bank to lend to businesses and individuals to stimulate economic activity.

In the United States, the FRB conducted three rounds of QE between 2008 and 2014, purchasing a total of $4.5 trillion in assets. This increase in the money supply helped stimulate economic growth.
Japan has also implemented a large-scale QE program in recent years, aimed at fighting deflation and boosting economic growth.

The Bank of Japan has been buying assets such as government bonds since 2013, and this increase in the money supply has helped the country fight off deflation. Critics of QE argue that it can lead to inflation and asset bubbles because an increase in the money supply can lead to excess demand and higher prices.
However, supporters argue that QE is an essential tool for central banks to use in times of economic difficulty, and that risks can be managed through careful implementation and monitoring.

5. Modern Monetary Theory (MMT)
Modern Monetary Theory (MMT) is an economic theory that has gained popularity in recent years following the global financial crisis of 2008-09. It was promoted by a group of economists, including Stephanie Kelton, Warren Mosler, and L. Randall Ray, who sought to challenge traditional views of government finance and debt.

Definition.
MMT essentially argues that a government that issues its own currency can never run out of money, and that its spending is not limited by taxes or borrowing.
In other words, the government can print money at will to finance its spending without relying on tax revenues or bond sales to fund its activities.

Means
According to MMT, a government can create new money through deficit financing, which is the difference between what the government spends and what it collects in taxes.
When a government spends more money than it collects in taxes, it creates a deficit, which injects new money into the economy.

This in turn creates jobs and stimulates economic activity.
MMT argues that deficit spending is not inherently bad and can be used to achieve important policy goals such as full employment, stable prices, and economic growth.

Examples
One of the most prominent examples of MMT is Japan, which has been running large fiscal deficits for decades, and its debt-to-GDP ratio is currently around 240%, the highest in the developed world.
According to traditional economic theory, Japan should face high inflation and interest rates, and its economy should struggle, but Japan has experienced years of low inflation and low interest rates, and its economy has been stable.

Thus, MMT advocates point to Japan as an example of how a government that issues its own currency can use it to achieve its policy goals through deficit financing without facing the funding limitations of households or businesses.
In Japan's case, the government was able to finance its spending by issuing bonds that were largely bought by domestic investors.

This kept interest rates low and allowed the government to continue deficit spending without facing a debt crisis.
Japan also favored fiscal spending based on MMT theory over monetary policy because it was more in line with the intentions of Japanese officials, who saw fiscal policy as having a simple, direct effect and being easier to understand than monetary policy, which was more difficult and had longer repercussions due to political factors such as vested interests in the Ministry of Finance.

Critics of MMT argue that the theory is overly simplistic and does not take into account the potential risks of deficit spending, such as inflation and loss of confidence in the currency.
However, MMT proponents argue that these risks can be managed through taxation and bond issuance, and that inflation can be controlled if the currency can be exported through foreign demand.

MMT challenges traditional views of government finance and debt, arguing that a government that issues its own currency can never run out of money and that deficit spending can be used to achieve important policy goals.
However, it remains to be seen whether it will work outside of countries with the economic power to issue their own currency, such as the United States and Japan.

6. Differences in the use of monetary policy tools between QE and MMT
Modern monetary theory (MMT) and monetary policy instruments such as quantitative easing, open market operations, discount rate policy, and interest rate policy entail the management of a country's money supply and economy, but they differ in approach and purpose.

Quantitative easing (QE)

QE is a monetary policy in which a central bank injects money into the financial system to stimulate the economy.

Typically, the central bank buys government bonds or other securities from banks, and the banks that receive the liquidity provide more liquidity by lending to businesses and individuals.

The goal is to lower interest rates to increase borrowing and investment and stimulate economic growth, and QE is a common tool used to combat deflation or recession.

In contrast, MMT does not rely on QE to stimulate the economy, instead arguing that governments can create money to finance spending without causing inflation.

It argues that governments are not constrained by the need to borrow money because they can simply create new currency to support their spending.

This approach is based on the belief that the money supply is not fixed and that the government has the power to create or destroy money at will.

Open Market Operations (OMO)

Open market operation policy (OMO) is when a central bank buys and sells government bonds or other securities in the open market, which affects the supply of liquidity.

When a central bank buys securities, it increases the money supply, and when it sells securities, it decreases the money supply. The operational goals of open market manipulation policies are to maintain stable prices, promote full employment, and stabilize the economy.

MMT also recognizes the use of open market manipulation policies, but suggests that they are unnecessary for government spending.

MMT argues that in the government bond market, the central bank can achieve better monetary spillovers by reducing the process and time through direct acquisitions.

Discount rate policy

The discount rate is the rate at which banks borrow money from the central bank. By changing the discount rate, the central bank can affect borrowing costs and the money supply.

When the discount rate is low, borrowing is cheaper and more money is available for lending, which can stimulate the economy.

MMT does not focus on interest rates as a tool to control the economy. Instead, it emphasizes the role of government spending in creating jobs and stimulating economic activity.

MMT argues that governments can create jobs directly, rather than relying on the private sector, to ensure that everyone who wants a job has one.

Interest rate policy

Interest rate policy refers to the setting of interest rates by central banks to influence the supply and demand for credit in an economy.

Lower interest rates can stimulate economic growth by encouraging borrowing and investment. Conversely, higher interest rates can discourage borrowing and investment and help control inflation.

MMT takes a different approach to interest rates, arguing that they are not the primary driver of economic activity.

Instead, MMT argues that government spending is the key to maintaining full employment and stable prices. Interest rates are viewed as a tool that can be used to manage borrowing costs, not as a primary mechanism to control inflation or encourage growth.

MMT and traditional monetary policy measures differ in their approach and goals. While traditional monetary policy tools focus on managing the money supply and interest rates to stabilize the economy, MMT emphasizes the role of government fiscal spending in creating jobs and stimulating economic activity.

The first corporation emerges

For nearly three centuries, from the early 15th to the mid-18th century, European ships roamed the globe, carving out routes, exploring and trading, a period known as the Age of Exploration.

Items such as porcelain from China and spices from India were popular commodities with returns in excess of 10,000 percent, but the Ottoman Empire's control of the Middle East in the 16th century made it difficult to trade overland, so traders turned to the sea.

During this time, the English and Dutch competed for maritime rights, with the English defeating the Spanish Armada in 1588 and establishing a monopoly on the sea, while the Dutch fought an 80-year war of independence against Spain beginning in 1566 over the suppression of Protestantism.

Even during the War of Independence, Dutch merchants pioneered routes, including the establishment of the Indonesian sea route in 1595, and established the spice trade, the most important trade commodity of the time.

Especially in the 16th and 17th centuries, European nations were expanding their territories and establishing colonies around the world. To finance these projects, they pitched them to private investors and promised them a share of the profits.

These investors were usually organized in the form of joint stock companies that allowed them to share in the risks and rewards of the investment.

The British East India Company (EIC) was founded in 1600, two years before the Dutch East India Company(VOC, Verenig de Oostindische Compagnie), and was granted a trade monopoly in the East Indies by Queen Elizabeth I. The EIC was not a public company.

However, the EIC did not issue shares to the public and was much smaller than the VOC. Unlike the VOC, the EIC did not have a monopoly on trade in Asia. Nevertheless, the EIC played an important role in the expansion of the British Empire and contributed to the colonization of India.

The EIC's initial financing was one-time, raising money each time a ship set sail, selling goods from overseas, and distributing the proceeds to investors in proportion to their investment. If the ship didn't make it back safely, it would be wiped out with no dividends.

This investment structure was risky and made it difficult for the company to exist as a going concern. The Dutch East India Company, known as the Verenig de Oostindische Compagnie (VOC), was founded in the Netherlands in 1602 and was the first company to issue shares to the general public, and it quickly grew to become the largest trading company in the world.

The VOC realized that they could not survive as a going concern with the same financing structure as the EIC. They looked for ways to spread the risk and allow investors to invest less money, which led to the development of the stock.

In 1606, the Dutch East India Company (VOC) issued stock receipts that proved how much an investor had invested in the company, which evolved into stock ownership. The VOC monopolized trade between the Netherlands and Asia and dominated the spice trade in the 17th and 18th centuries.

The company was granted broad powers by the Dutch government to wage war, negotiate treaties, and establish colonies.

The difference between the two companies is the political and economic context in which they were founded. The Netherlands was a republic, which meant that power was decentralized, and there was a tradition of entrepreneurship and trade.

In addition, rather than having a feudal aristocracy in a feudalized region like Spain, the newly independent country had a low percentage of aristocrats and a large number of merchants engaged in overseas trade, creating an entrepreneurial culture based on mercantilism.

This allowed creative institutions like the joint stock company to emerge.

In contrast, England was a monarchy with a more centralized government and a less developed commercial sector.

While the Dutch government supported VOCs and gave them considerable power, the English government was more cautious about empowering private companies.

In 1609, the sale of shares to other investors was authorized, and the first stock exchange was established in Amsterdam to facilitate the trading of VOC shares. Seventeen of VOC's investors, including founder Dirk Vass, reportedly made more than 80 times their investment. During Tulipmania, especially in the Netherlands, VOC's stock rose and fell with the price of tulips.

However, while tulips were overpriced relative to their intrinsic value and crashed, never to regain their peak price, VOC's stock remained stable even after the tulip bubble burst, providing investors with steady profits and dividends.

The exchange allowed investors to buy and sell shares of the company, which gave the stock liquidity and helped increase its value.

The success of the VOC and the establishment of the stock exchange contributed to the development of Amsterdam as a financial center.

However, by the late 18th century, when the VOC began to decay internally and the Netherlands began to lose its disaster rights due to competition from other European powers, it began to decline due to declining profits.

Eventually, the VOC was dissolved in 1800, ending its long life of 200 years.

In the United States, banks and transportation companies began to emerge as corporations in the late 18th and early 19th centuries.

The rise of corporations was largely due to the economic growth of the United States and the need for financial and transportation infrastructure, with banks and transportation companies emerging first because they were necessary for the expansion of trade and commerce.

However, it wasn't until the late 19th century that a legal framework for corporations was established in the United States.

This legal framework provided corporations with limited liability and other legal protections, allowing entrepreneurs to start and grow their businesses without fear of personal financial ruin.

One of the most important laws that gave businesses limited liability and other legal protections was the Limited Liability Act of 1855.

This act allowed for the formation of limited liability companies (LLCs).

LLCs gave limited liability to their owners, meaning that owners were only liable for the company's debts up to the amount they had invested.

This protection allowed entrepreneurs to take risks without putting their personal assets at risk.

Another important law that legally protected businesses was the Sherman Antitrust Act of 1890. It was designed to prevent monopolies and promote competition in the marketplace.

It prohibited certain business practices, such as price-fixing and agreements to divide markets between competitors. The Securities Act of 1933 and the Securities Exchange Act of 1934 also played an important role in creating legal protections for businesses.

These laws required companies to disclose certain financial information to investors and provide other protections, such as the right to sue for securities fraud.

The first joint-stock company in Korea was the Chosun Bank (closed in 1901), founded in 1896. This was followed by the establishment of the Bukhara Railroad Company in 1898, the Korea Cheon Il Bank and the Korea Railroad Company in 1899, and other financial institutions such as the Hansung Agricultural and Industrial Bank in 1906 and the Dongyang Chuksik Corporation in 1908.

Currency and the gold standard

The concept of money dates back to ancient civilizations like Mesopotamia and Egypt, where people used commodities like gold and silver as a medium of exchange.

Over time, as societies became more complex, attempts were made to standardize currency, and governments began issuing paper money backed by precious metals like gold and silver.

However, the currency used for trade and commerce was replaced by various objects. One example is the use of salt as a form of currency.

In ancient times, salt was a very valuable commodity because it was used not only for seasoning but also for preserving food. In fact, the word "salary" comes from the Latin word salarium, which originally referred to the amount of money paid to Roman soldiers to buy salt.

In some parts of the world, salt has been used as a form of currency for centuries. In West Africa, large bars of salt called amoles were used as a medium of exchange, and in Tibet, salt was traded for goods like tea and horses.

Another example of using goods instead of money is the barter system. In a barter system, goods or services are exchanged directly for other goods or services without using money.

For example, a farmer might trade a cow for a horse, or a baker might trade bread for milk. Barter was common in many ancient societies and is still used in some parts of the world today.

One example of the use of metals as currency is Lydia, located in present-day western Turkestan. It first used coins made of gold and silver around 650 B.C. These coins were valuable, portable, and standardized, making them a convenient medium of exchange.

Mesopotamia, in what is now Iraq, used a metric system to facilitate trade around 3,000 BC.

They used silver rings as a form of currency that could be weighed and verified. The ancient Greeks used a variety of currencies over the centuries, including metal coins such as gold, silver, and bronze coins, which were used not only for trade and commerce but also to pay taxes and other debts.

The first Greek coins were made of electrum (green gold), a natural alloy of gold and silver, and were used around the 7th century BC.

Over time, the Greeks began minting coins with images of gods, heroes, and animals, which became more elaborate and detailed over the centuries.

Greek coins were widely used throughout the Mediterranean and beyond, and played an important role in the growth of ancient Greek trade and commerce. The use of coins allowed for efficient trade and economic growth, which helped fuel the cultural and intellectual achievements of ancient Greece.

Gold was used as money early on for many reasons, one of the main ones being that it is a rare and precious metal, making it valuable and desirable as a medium of exchange.

It was also practical and convenient because it was durable, easily detachable, and easily transportable.

Gold does not corrode or tarnish, and it is easily identifiable and distinguishable from other metals, making it difficult to counterfeit. The scarcity and desirability of gold meant that it retained its value over time, making it a stable medium of exchange.

The use of gold as a currency dates back thousands of years and was used by many ancient civilizations, including the Egyptians, Greeks, and Romans. In modern times, gold has been used as a standard for international currency exchange, with the value of other currencies pegged to the value of gold.

This is known as the gold standard, under which paper currencies were redeemable for a fixed amount of gold.

The gold standard was first introduced in the 19th century and became the dominant monetary system around the world until 1971, when President

Nixon of the United States officially announced the end of the gold standard.

Here's a look at when major countries adopted the gold standard.
The United Kingdom
The gold standard was first introduced in the United Kingdom in 1816 due to economic instability and inflation caused by the Napoleonic Wars.
The British pound was pegged to gold at a rate of 4.25 pounds per ounce of gold, and the introduction of the gold standard helped stabilize the British economy and solidify the country's position as an economic and financial powerhouse.

The United States
The United States officially adopted the gold standard in 1900 after decades of debate and experimentation with other monetary systems.
The value of the U.S. dollar was pegged to gold at a rate of $20.67 per ounce of gold, and the gold standard helped establish the U.S. dollar as a stable and reliable currency, contributing to the growth of the U.S. economy in the early 20th century.

Germany
Germany adopted the gold standard in 1871 after unification. The German mark was pegged to gold at a rate of 2,790 marks per kilogram of gold. The introduction of this system helped to stabilize the German economy and establish Germany as a major economic power in Europe.

France
France adopted the gold standard in 1878 after decades of experimentation with other monetary systems. The French franc was pegged to gold at a rate of 1,550 francs per kilogram of gold. The gold standard helped stabilize the French economy and solidify France's position as a major financial center.

Japan
Japan adopted the gold standard in 1897 after decades of economic and political turmoil. The Japanese yen was pegged to gold at a rate of 2.48 pounds per gram of gold. This helped to stabilize the Japanese economy and establish the yen as a stable and reliable currency.

Proponents of the gold standard argued that it provided a stable and predictable monetary system because the value of a currency was tied to a fixed amount of gold.
This prevented governments from printing too much money and causing inflation.
In addition, the gold standard facilitated international trade and commerce

because countries could exchange currencies with the confidence that they would maintain a stable value.

The first gold standard and monetary exchanges were based on a fixed exchange rate between gold and paper money. Under the gold standard, the value of paper money was directly linked to the value of gold, meaning that paper money could be converted into a fixed amount of gold at a set price.

For example, if a country was on a gold standard and set the price of gold at $20 per ounce, paper money could be exchanged for gold based on that fixed exchange rate. This meant that the amount of paper money in circulation was limited by the amount of gold held by the country's central bank.

The use of the gold standard helped ensure the stability and predictability of the monetary system because it provided a tangible, universally recognized asset to back the value of paper money.

However, the gold standard also had its limitations. The supply of gold was limited, which meant that the money supply was also limited, which could limit economic growth. In addition, the fixed exchange rates under the gold standard made it difficult for governments to respond to changing economic conditions.

The gold standard began to decline in the early 20th century and was officially abandoned by the United States in 1971.

The process of abandoning the gold standard was gradual, with different countries taking different approaches.

Some countries, like the United States, abandoned the gold standard gradually over several years, while others, like the United Kingdom, abandoned it more abruptly.

After overspending in World War I, Britain and France temporarily abandoned the gold standard and increased the amount of their currency to pay for the war. After the war ended, they prepared to return to the gold standard when the wartime monetary loosening caused economic instability, including inflation.

However, inflation and the depreciation of its currency, the pound, meant that when Britain returned to the gold standard in 1925, the exchange rate of $4.86 per pound was overvalued in terms of the pound. Therefore, it was necessary to increase the value of the pound in order to maintain the gold standard.

The British government needed to raise interest rates to reduce the supply of pounds in circulation and attract gold back into the country.

Then, with the cooperation of the U.S. government, they got the U.S. to lower interest rates, which allowed gold to flow into the U.K. from the U.S. and cause the value of the British pound to appreciate against the U.S. dollar.

The British government also introduced austerity measures to reduce government spending and balance the budget. This was done to create a balance of payments surplus, reducing the supply of money in circulation and allowing the government to build up its gold reserves.

However, the overvalued pound made British exports more expensive in other countries, which led to a decline in British exports, and economic activity stagnated in the wake of a shrinking money supply and the Great Depression that was gripping the world at the time.
In addition, the fixed exchange rate system at the time made it difficult for the government to pursue independent monetary policy, which limited its ability to respond to changing economic conditions. These factors eventually led to Britain's abandonment of the gold standard in 1931.

France abandoned the gold standard during World War I due to the need to finance the war. The French government had to borrow a lot of money to finance the war, which led to inflation and a decline in the value of its currency, the franc.
To restore confidence in the franc and stabilize its price, the French government adopted a policy of pegging the franc to the value of gold in 1926, known as the "gold franc" policy.
Under this policy, the exchange rate of the franc was fixed at 0.134 francs per U.S. dollar, which is equivalent to 0.017 grams of gold per franc.

This represented a significant devaluation of the franc from the pre-World War I exchange rate of 0.2903 grams of gold per franc. The devaluation of the franc against gold was about 94%.
The "gold franc" policy succeeded in stabilizing the French economy and restoring confidence in the franc. The 94% devaluation of the franc also made French exports more competitive, which contributed to a trade surplus and the accumulation of gold reserves.

By the end of 1928, France's gold reserves had grown to 7.5 billion francs, more than 60% of the total gold reserves held by all central banks in the world.
However, this policy also created tensions with other countries in the international monetary system, especially the United States.
At the time, the United States was experiencing an economic boom and was importing more than it was exporting, leading to a trade deficit. This was the case with the United States and Japan during the Plaza Agreement, when Japan's devaluation widened the U.S. trade deficit.

However, the war reparations owed to France by Germany, the victor of World War I, did not come in, and the U.S. and the U.K. cooperated on interest rates, setting low interest rates in the U.S. and high interest rates in the U.K., causing U.S. gold to move to the U.K. and causing France to have difficulty securing gold.

These factors eventually led to a shortage of gold reserves and the devaluation of the franc in 1936. In particular, the Great Depression that began in 1929 led to the abandonment of the gold standard in the 1930s because it was believed that the restrictions on the money supply imposed by the gold standard contributed to the severity of the crisis.
In order to rectify this chaotic international monetary order, which saw the abandonment and return of the gold standard, a conference was held in Bretton Woods, New Hampshire, USA, in 1944, near the end of World War II, where the Bretton Woods system was designed.

The goal of the conference was to create a new international monetary system that would promote economic stability and growth by regulating exchange rates and providing a framework for international trade and investment. Under the Bretton Woods system, the U.S. dollar was chosen as the world's reserve currency, and other currencies were pegged to the U.S. dollar at a fixed exchange rate.
The U.S. dollar was linked to gold at a fixed rate of $35 per ounce, and countries other than the United States linked their currencies to the U.S. dollar.

This system was designed to provide stability to exchange rates and limit inflation because the supply of currency was tied to a country's gold reserves.
The Bretton Woods system was ultimately intended to correct the international monetary order by linking gold to the dollar under the gold standard and the currencies of all countries except the United States to the dollar.
This system remained in place until President Nixon abandoned the gold standard in 1971, and it served to maintain an effective global monetary order.

However, because of the dollar's prominent role in the Bretton Woods system, it was difficult to maintain the system when the dollar became overused.
The excessive costs of the U.S. war in Vietnam raised concerns about the U.S. dollar, and in 1971 the U.S. abandoned the gold standard in the Bretton Woods system.

The U.S. abandonment of the gold standard was a gradual process that took place over several decades.
In 1933, President Franklin Roosevelt issued an executive order requiring all

Americans to surrender gold coins, bullion, and certificates to the Federal Reserve in exchange for paper currency.

This move effectively made it illegal for private citizens to own gold, and helped the government increase its gold reserves.

In 1934, Congress passed the Gold Reserve Act, which authorized the government to fix the price of gold and issue paper money that was not backed by gold.

This was quite controversial because it allowed the government to increase the money supply without increasing its gold reserves.

In 1944, the United States attended the Bretton Woods Conference to establish a new world monetary system based on the U.S. dollar.

In this Bretton Woods system, the value of the U.S. dollar was pegged to gold at a rate of $35 per ounce of gold, and other currencies were pegged to the U.S. dollar.

By 1971, the U.S. was faced with a protracted Vietnam War, which led to increased printing of U.S. dollars and government deficits that led to inflation and a decline in the value of the U.S. dollar.

At the same time, the U.S. was running a large trade deficit, and under the gold standard, foreign investors demanded that U.S. dollars be exchanged for U.S. gold. The U.S. exchanged dollars for gold and exported gold in large quantities.

As the U.S. government's gold reserves began to dwindle, there was growing concern among foreign governments and investors that the U.S. would not be able to honor its promise to exchange dollars for gold at a fixed rate of $35 per ounce.

In addition, many economists and policymakers began to question the usefulness of the gold standard as a means of regulating the global economy.

Some argued that the fixed exchange rate between gold and paper money was too rigid and prevented governments from pursuing monetary policies that could help stabilize their economies.

Eventually, in August 1971, U.S. President Richard Nixon announced that the United States would no longer honor its commitment to exchange U.S. dollars for gold at a fixed rate of $35 per ounce.

This action ended the Bretton Woods system that had been in place since the end of World War II and marked an important transition to fiat currencies.

Since then, the value of the U.S. dollar and other currencies has been determined by market forces and investor confidence in the issuing government. The impact of abandoning the gold standard was profound.

In the short term, the value of the U.S. dollar fell sharply as investors rushed to sell their dollars in exchange for other currencies and goods.

In the long run, the move away from the gold standard allowed the U.S. government greater flexibility in managing the economy because it was no longer tied to a fixed exchange rate backed by gold.

Once the United States decided to leave the gold standard, other countries followed suit.

Exchange rate and trade issues with the U.S. led to a global shift away from gold in favor of the dollar, and the dollar's acceptance by oil-producing nations such as Saudi Arabia played a large role in this shift.

A society in which economic activities are carried out only by government-issued currency, not linked to gold or silver, has long been the ideal of governments.

Governments established central banks to issue money and wanted to create an unlimited supply of money.

However, it was not possible to implement a fully gold- or silver-backed (modern monetary system that is not redeemable for money) system because people in the economy did not recognize the value of paper bills or copper coins that were not backed by anything of value such as gold or silver.

Due to problems with trust in governments and central banks, and the negative effects of over-issued money that was not tied to gold, such as depreciation and inflation when costs spiked due to war, gold and silver convertibility policies were maintained for a long time despite the desire of governments to abandon them.

Historically, there have been instances of temporary abandonment of the gold standard and the use of greenbacks to pay for excessive war expenses or to solve national debt problems, such as Lincoln's temporary abandonment of the gold standard and the use of greenbacks, and John Law's issuance of unredeemable notes by the Banque Royale, the French central bank, but the process of returning to the gold standard has always been a gradual one.

Thus, President Nixon's announcement in 1971 that he would abandon the gold standard and gold convertibility and introduce a monetary system backed solely by the credit of the government was a major event in human economic history.

The economic power of the United States grew to the point that the dollar was recognized as the world's reserve currency, meaning that the dollar was recognized as a medium of exchange as valuable as gold or silver.

However, there was a concern that the dollar's status as a reserve currency increased the likelihood that the economic crisis in the United States would be contagious to the rest of the world.

The famous economist Keynes was concerned about this and advocated for a separate world currency.

However, the abolition of the gold standard did not stop the flood of fiat money, and preventing cyclical inflation became a priority for governments around the world.

Due to the nature of gold as a scarce resource, the money supply was limited under the gold standard, which had the effect of suppressing inflation and even triggering deflation.

As a result, the idea of increasing the supply of money by implementing a silver standard, or a system that combines the gold standard with a relatively large reserve of silver, has been a perennial suggestion from government officials in times of war and other costly expenditures.

Historically, however, there have been many instances where wars have resulted in an oversupply of currency or bubbles caused by speculation over scarce resources, so the gold standard has long been a stalwart reserve currency.

However, the gold standard has been abandoned, and the role of careful, micro-prudential monetary and interest rate policies and supervisory authorities has become crucial to overcoming its adverse effects.

The impact of the end of the gold standard is still debated by economists today. Some argue that the shift to fiat currencies has contributed to greater financial stability and economic growth, while others argue that it has increased volatility and uncertainty in the global economy.

Conflict over the adoption of the gold and silver standards in China

China traditionally practiced a monetary system based on the silver standard, which was widely practiced for centuries and was also widely used in other parts of Asia.

The silver standard was based on a fixed exchange rate between silver and paper money. In China, the silver tael was the standard unit of currency, and one tael (about 50 grams in 1959 Chinese currency) was equivalent to a fixed amount of banknotes.

The exchange rate between silver coins and paper money was set by the government and was generally stable and predictable.

The advantages of using silver as a currency are that it is more easily separated than gold, making it convenient for smaller transactions; it is more abundant than gold in quantity, making it cheaper and more accessible; and it is easier to measure and weigh, making it easier to determine value.

On the downside, silver is less durable than gold and can corrode over time; it is heavier than gold, making it inconvenient to transport and trade; and because it is more abundant than gold, its value may be more susceptible to inflation and price fluctuations.

Because of these characteristics, the silver standard could be implemented using basic accounting and bookkeeping practices and helped many people to engage in economic activity.

By the late 19th century, China was facing significant economic and political challenges, including the decline of the Qing dynasty, the rise of Western imperialism, and the influx of foreign goods and currencies, and was torn between the gold standard favored by Western powers and the traditional silver standard.

At the time, China was a major producer of silver, and the country had a long history of using silver as currency. Many Chinese officials believed that the adoption of a gold standard would be disadvantageous to China because it would lead to a decline in the price of silver and a loss of competitiveness in international trade.

China was also facing pressure from Western powers to adopt the gold standard as part of a policy of economic and political reform.

Some Chinese officials viewed the adoption of the gold standard as a form of Western imperialism and believed it undermined China's sovereignty and economic independence.

In addition, the gold standard required an advanced banking and financial system, which China did not have at the time.

Many Chinese officials believed that adopting the gold standard would be difficult and costly, requiring significant investment in new infrastructure and technology, and preferred to stick with the silver standard rather than the gold standard.

The conflict between the gold and silver standards peaked in the early 20th century when China was forced to borrow heavily from foreign powers to finance its military and economic modernization.

The resulting debt crisis and political instability continued after the fall of the Qing Dynasty and the establishment of the Republic of China in 1912.

In 1935, a global silver price crash led to significant inflation and currency instability in China. In response, the Chinese government officially abandoned the silver standard and introduced a new currency, the yuan.
However, as inflation and economic instability continued, the Chinese government experimented with a gold standard. In 1935, the Chinese government established the Central Bank of China and announced that it would begin using gold as a reserve asset to back the value of the yuan.
The yuan was exchanged for gold at a fixed rate, and the central bank was responsible for stockpiling gold to back the currency.

While the gold standard experiment succeeded in stabilizing the yuan and restoring confidence, the lack of infrastructure and resources to support a gold-based monetary system made the experiment a failure, and in 1936, China abandoned the gold standard and returned to the silver standard.

Several factors contributed to the failure of the gold standard experiment, including
1. Insufficient gold reserves
China did not have enough gold to back the yuan, and the government was unable to secure enough gold to back the value of the yuan.

2. Lack of international support
The global economic and political climate in the 1930s was not favorable to the gold standard, and China struggled to find support from other countries for its monetary policy.

3. Weak banking system

China's banking system was underdeveloped and lacked the resources and infrastructure necessary to support a gold-based monetary system.

After the Chinese Communist Party won the Nationalist Civil War in 1949, China underwent significant changes to its monetary system.

The new communist government sought to establish a centrally planned economy, which required a highly centralized monetary system.

This required the abolition of the silver standard and monetary reforms that had been in place until then.

In 1955, the People's Bank of China issued a new currency, the renminbi, to replace the old yuan. The renminbi was initially issued as banknotes, with denominations ranging from 1 pen to 1,000 yuan.

From this point on, the new currency was off the silver standard and became a fiat currency, meaning that its value was preserved and did not fluctuate with the price of certain commodities. The Chinese government was able to exercise greater control over the money supply and use monetary policy to manage the economy.

In 1955, the Chinese government also revalued its currency, setting the exchange rate against the U.S. dollar at 2.46 yuan. This marked a significant increase in the value of the yuan and helped stabilize the currency and restore confidence in the country's monetary system.

In 1957, the Chinese government began phasing out silver coins, replacing them with copper-nickel alloy coins.

This helped to decouple the currency from the silver standard and reduce the country's dependence on silver as a commodity.

Overall, the process of abolishing the silver standard in China was a policy of the Chinese Communist Party to modernize and centralize the Chinese economy.

It helped create a more stable and controllable monetary system by moving away from the silver standard.

The conflict between the gold and silver standards in the United States, and the Wizard of Oz.

During the American Revolutionary War, the independent government issued currency to pay for the war, but it became obsolete due to the lack of trust in the government and officially used a bullion system using both gold and silver.

Then, in 1834, after the first and second attempts to establish and stabilize a central bank failed, the U.S. Congress changed the ratio of gold to silver from 1:15 to 1:16, and gold became the primary means of currency.

Although President Lincoln briefly abolished the gold standard and used a fiat currency called "greenbacks" to raise money for the Civil War, after the Civil War, the gold standard and the silver standard coexisted in parallel.

However, the conflict between the gold and silver standards in the United States was a major economic and political issue in the late 19th century.
The issue of the relative value and exchange rate of gold and silver was a major point of contention.
Proponents of the gold standard argued that gold was more stable and reliable than silver, and that it should be the primary standard for national currencies.

They also believed that using too much silver to back a currency could lead to inflation and economic instability.
On the other hand, proponents of the silver standard argued that silver was more abundant and accessible than gold and should be used more extensively to back a nation's currency.

They also believed that using more silver would help stimulate economic growth and reduce the power of wealthy elites to control the gold supply. Throughout the late 19th and early 20th centuries, the United States used both gold and silver as the basis of its currency.

The exchange rate between gold and silver was fixed by law, which was quite controversial.
When large fluctuations in the gold-silver exchange rate and uncertainty in the value of the currency led to economic instability and uncertainty, the U.S. Congress passed the Gold Standard Act of 1873, facing significant opposition from supporters of the silver standard.

In 1879, the U.S. government introduced the Gold Standard Policy, which aimed to address the problems associated with the transition to the gold standard. Under this policy, the government agreed to purchase large quantities of silver each month and issue silver certificates that could be used as legal tender in the same way as gold certificates.

In 1900, the Gold Standard Act was passed, making gold the sole standard for money and effectively ending the use of silver as a standard.

As the production of gold decreased and the supply of money tied to it decreased, deflation set in, causing prices, especially for agricultural products, to fall, prompting farmers to call for the return of the silver standard.

Here's an example of how farmers and debtors were harmed by the deflationary effects of the gold standard.

For example, suppose that in 1895, a wheat farmer in the United States earned $10,000 in agricultural profits, paying off a $4,000 loan and keeping $6,000 in his pocket.

If we assume that the production of gold decreased in 1896, reducing the supply of dollars under the gold standard, we would expect the value of the dollar to increase and the price of agricultural commodities to decrease, reducing agricultural profits to $9,000.

However, the $4,000 loan would remain unchanged, and the farmer would have a net income of $5,000.
However, a parallel monetary system with a silver standard, increasing the supply of silver alongside the scarce gold, could protect against deflation, or it could cause inflation and increase the profitability of agricultural products.
The farmer would be able to keep more of his net income because the currency would be worth less and his profits would increase, but his debt would remain unchanged.

If not more, he can at least expect to have no less net income than the previous year. For this reason, peasants rejected the gold standard, which caused deflation, in favor of bimetallism, a system in which both the gold and silver standards are compatible.

The idea of a silver standard, which would base money on the increasingly abundant silver instead of the less abundant gold, became popular among farmers whose incomes had fallen due to deflation, and presidential candidates began to appear who advocated a silver standard.

In 1896, William Jennings Bryan advocated for a silver standard during his presidential campaign.

Claiming that the gold standard was a "Cross of Gold" that oppressed humanity, Bryan advocated for a silver standard, while other conservative presidential candidates stuck to the gold standard.

At the time, the United States was on the gold standard, which meant that the country's currency was tied to it. Many businesses and financiers supported the gold standard because they believed it maintained economic stability and protected their interests.

Bryan, a young Democratic politician from Nebraska, supported the silver standard and emerged as a strong advocate for the interests of farmers and other working-class Americans.

His famous "Cross of Gold" speech at the 1896 Democratic National Convention captured the nation's attention and boosted his popularity.
His famous Cross of Gold speech is known as an impassioned defense of bimetallism, a monetary system that allows for the free minting of gold and silver.

In the speech, Bryan argued that the gold standard adopted by the United States in 1873 had created a deflationary spiral, hurting farmers and other debtors.

By restricting the money supply and tying the value of the U.S. dollar to gold, he argued, the government was effectively enriching its creditors at the expense of its debtors.
The solution to this problem, Bryan argued, was to expand the money supply by allowing the free minting of silver in a fixed ratio to gold.

Bryan's speech included the famous phrase "You shall not crucify mankind upon a cross of gold," which became a rallying cry for proponents of the gold standard.

He argued that the gold standard was a tool used by the rich and powerful to maintain their economic dominance over the rest of society. He urged the Democratic Party to embrace the gold standard as a way to promote economic justice and equality.

Although Bryan was unsuccessful in winning the Democratic presidential nomination that year, his speech helped to popularize the issue of the gold standard and eventually paved the way for the adoption of the Gold Standard Act of 1900. The speech is remembered as one of the most iconic and influential in American political history.

Despite facing significant opposition from the business community and the Republican Party, Bryan's message resonated with many Americans, especially in the agricultural centers of the Midwest and South.

He campaigned vigorously, crisscrossing the country, speaking to large crowds and mobilizing grassroots support. Although Bryan received a lot of support from the business community, he lost to William McKinley, who had far more financial resources.

The Wizard of Oz is a work of fiction written by William Baum against the backdrop of these political debates. In The Wizard of Oz, Frank Baum uses various characters and symbols to represent the political and economic issues of the time, including the conflict between the gold and silver standards.

Here's a brief plot synopsis

There was a girl named Dorothy who lived in a lonely house in the middle of a vast plain. One day, a tornado, a great whirlwind, blew her house into the land of Oz, and Dorothy decided to visit the Great Wizard of the Emerald City to find her way back home.

On her way, she met the Scarecrow, who wanted to be smart, the Tin Man, who needed a heart, and the Cowardly Lion, and together they went to see the Wizard of Oz.

The Wizard of Oz agreed to grant them all their wishes if they could defeat the Wicked Witch of the West.

Along the way, they were attacked by wolves and bees, but Dorothy and her friends worked together to defeat the Wicked Witch of the West and return to the Emerald City.

The Wizard of Oz rewarded the Scarecrow with a brain, the Tin Man with a heart, and the Lion with courage.

And Dorothy was able to return home safely, thanks to the heel of her silver slipper.

『The Wizard of Oz on stage (Source: Wikimedia Commons)』

In The Wizard of Oz, Oz represents the ounce, the unit of measure for weighing gold and silver, Dorothy represents the average American citizen, and the headless scarecrow represents the farmers who struggled under the gold standard.

The tin man without a heart represents the auto workers who suffered under the gold standard, and the lion without courage represents the political leaders who lacked the courage to take action and change the system.

The western whirlwind represents the bimetallism craze in the American West, while the yellow brick road Dorothy walks on with her silver shoes represents the gold standard and her silver shoes represent the silver standard.

The Wicked Witch of the East and the Wicked Witch of the West both refer to political forces that opposed the combination of the two gold and silver standards at the time. Dorothy wears her silver shoes to help peasants, laborers, and others on her journey to defeat the bad witches.

The good witch says, "The silver shoes you're wearing will take you over the desert." This is an allusion to the theme that the silver standard, along with the gold standard, will get the country through this recession and deflation.

Under the gold standard, the deflationary problems caused by the lack of gold production were somewhat solved by the development of gold mines in South

Africa and Alaska, and the gold standard was reestablished. It remained in place until President Nixon abolished the gold standard in 1971.

How the dollar became a reserve currency

The process of the US dollar becoming a reserve currency began in the late 19th and early 20th centuries, but accelerated during World War I and World War II. The United States emerged as the economically and militarily superior power in both world wars, and its currency was increasingly used in international trade and finance.

During World War I, the United States was a major creditor to the Allies, providing credit and financial support to help sustain the war effort. This increased the use of the U.S. dollar in international trade because it was seen as a stable and reliable means of value.

After World War I, the United States emerged as a major creditor as countries around the world borrowed large amounts of money from American banks and investors. Since they needed dollars to pay off their debts, the demand for U.S. dollars in international finance was bound to increase.

This process continued during World War II, when the United States once again provided financial and military support to the Allies and emerged as the economic and military superpower after the war. The U.S. dollar's place on the gold standard was further solidified at the Bretton Woods Conference in 1944, when the dollar's value was established as a fixed exchange rate backed by gold.

And as U.S. aid programs began to work for war recovery, and the U.S. became the largest investor in European aid, Asian aid, as well as global aid programs, dollars became a global supply.
The dollar was also used to pay for oil, and as the global demand for oil increased, the supply of dollars increased, and no other currency could threaten the dollar.

The U.S. dollar has become the reserve currency for the following reasons
Economic strength
The United States emerged from World Wars I and II as the world's leading economic power, and its growing economy was able to support the use of the U.S. dollar in international trade and finance.
Its overwhelming economic power made it the largest donor to post-war reconstruction and aid programs, making the dollar a global currency.

The U.S. also currently has the world's largest trade deficit, meaning that it exported the most goods to the U.S. from countries other than the U.S., and those countries received dollars in return.
This creates a situation where the dollar is the most circulated and used

currency in the world.

Political Stability

The United States is recognized as a stable and reliable country with strong political institutions, rule of law, and a commitment to capitalism. This has made the US dollar a trusted currency for international transactions.

Political stability is a very important factor for a reserve currency. Some politically unstable countries have seen their exchange rates fluctuate wildly.

In the case of the United States, Congress has the power to vote on the federal government's debt limit, and there have been instances where the federal government has shut down due to conflicts with Congress.

This led to a downgrade of the U.S. credit rating and an increase in risk indicators such as CDS (Credit Default Swap).

This is an example of how political instability can affect the stability of a currency.

Military power

The United States has emerged as the world's leading military power since World War II and has established itself as the world's police state.

The Bretton Woods System

The fixed exchange rate system established at the Bretton Woods Conference helped solidify the US dollar's role as a reserve currency because it provided a stable framework for international trade and finance.

By fixing the exchange rate between the U.S. dollar and gold, as well as the dollar's exchange rate with the currencies of other countries, the Bretton Woods system formally recognized the dollar's reserve currency status.

The Petrodollar System

On October 17, 1973, Henry Kissinger delivered a speech at a National Press Club luncheon in Washington, DC. The speech came at a crucial moment in the world oil crisis, triggered by the oil embargo against countries that supported Israel in the Yom Kippur War.

In his speech, Kissinger recognized the gravity of the situation and called for a comprehensive diplomatic effort to resolve the crisis. He emphasized the importance of avoiding military confrontation in the region and finding a peaceful solution.

Kissinger also pointed to the lack of economic and political stability in the Middle East as the root cause of the crisis and the need to address it.

He proposed a long-term solution in which the United States would work with other industrialized nations to provide economic aid and support to the region's oil-producing countries.

The most important part of Kissinger's speech, however, was his proposal for a new international monetary system based on the value of oil. He proposed that the price of oil be calculated in a stable currency, such as the U.S. dollar, and that oil-producing countries invest their surplus revenues in U.S. banks.

In October 1973, U.S. Secretary of State Henry Kissinger held a series of secret meetings with the leaders of the major oil-producing countries in the Middle East.

The meetings were prompted by the Organization of Petroleum Exporting Countries (OPEC) oil embargo, which had been imposed in response to U.S. support for Israel during the Yom Kippur War, the fourth Middle East War.

At the meeting, Kissinger proposed that oil-producing countries pay for their oil in dollars and deposit their excess profits in U.S. banks.

In return, the United States offered to militarily protect the oil-producing countries and guarantee their security from external threats, a proposal that became known as the petrodollar system.

Behind the proposal was the U.S. calculation that it needed to maintain the value of the dollar against inflation caused by the Vietnam War and other factors. At the time, the U.S. dollar was the dominant currency internationally and was used to settle most international transactions.

The leaders of the oil-producing countries recognized and agreed to the proposal because it would provide a stable source of income for their economies. The agreement to pay for oil in dollars and invest surplus revenues in U.S. banks was a win-win for both the United States and the oil-producing countries. The United States maintained its economic and political influence in the Middle East, and the oil-producing countries gained a stable source of income and access to U.S. financial institutions.

Middle Eastern oil producers agreed to Kissinger's proposal for a new international monetary system based on the value of oil because it provided a stable source of revenue and access to U.S. financial institutions.

By tying the price of oil, which was in global demand, to the dollar, the United States could ensure a steady demand for its currency and print more dollars without worrying about inflation.

The decision to go with the petrodollar system had several effects.
First, it strengthened the United States' position as a global economic and military power.
By securing the petrodollar system, the United States was able to maintain the stability of the global financial system and protect its interests in the Middle East.

Second, the petrodollar system stimulated the U.S. economy by creating a constant demand for dollars.
This demand for dollars allowed the U.S. to address its fiscal deficit and trade imbalances without inflationary pressures.

Third, the petrodollar system also had a major impact on oil-producing countries in the Middle East. By pricing their oil in dollars and depositing excess profits in U.S. banks, these countries became increasingly dependent on the United States and vulnerable to changes in U.S. economic and political policies.

The geopolitical situation at the time, coupled with the global energy crisis caused by the Organization of the Petroleum Exporting Countries (OPEC) oil embargo, allowed Kissinger to make his proposal, which laid the groundwork for a petrodollar system that would ensure the U.S. dollar remained the dominant international currency and allow the United States to maintain its economic and political influence in the Middle East.

Network effects
Once the U.S. dollar became widely accepted for international transactions, it created network effects that made it more attractive to other countries and businesses, further increasing its use.
A specific example of a network effect that increased the use of the U.S. dollar in international transactions was the dollar's role in global commodity markets.

Because commodities like oil and gold are priced in U.S. dollars, countries and companies around the world needed to hold dollars to purchase these commodities.
As more countries and businesses began to use the U.S. dollar for commodity transactions, other countries and businesses found it more attractive to hold dollars, creating a network effect.

This, in turn, further increased the use of the US dollar in global trade and finance.
For example, if a country like Japan wants to buy oil from Saudi Arabia, it needs

U.S. dollars to pay for the oil, even if it doesn't produce or trade oil in the U.S. This creates a demand for U.S. dollars.

This creates demand for the U.S. dollar, strengthening the dollar's position as an international currency.

As more and more countries and businesses adopted the use of the U.S. dollar for international transactions, it became more attractive for other countries and businesses to do the same, creating a self-reinforcing cycle.

These network effects helped maintain the U.S. dollar's dominance in the global economy and gave the U.S. significant economic and political power.

The rise of the US dollar as a reserve currency was a complex and multifaceted process that was driven by economic, political, and military factors, as well as institutional frameworks such as the Bretton Woods system.

However, the dollar's position as a reserve currency has not always been secure. Both the yen and the euro have been viewed as potential challengers to the U.S. dollar's position as a reserve currency in the global economy.

The Chinese currency, the renminbi, is also growing in importance as an international currency, but it is not yet freely convertible and is not widely used in global trade and finance.

Here are some specific examples of how these currencies threaten the U.S. position as a reserve currency.

The Yen

Prior to the 1990s, the Japanese economy was booming and Japanese exports dominated the U.S. market. Some countries even used the yen as a reserve currency instead of the U.S. dollar to protect their industries.

For example, in 1989, Saudi Arabia announced that it would pay for oil in yen. This posed a significant threat to the dominance of the US dollar in the global economy. However, the development of the yen as an oil trading currency was limited for the following reasons.

First, the yen was not a freely convertible currency at the time, so it was not widely accepted in global trade and finance. This limited the ability of other countries to hold the yen as a reserve currency and use it to trade with other countries.

Second, Japan's central bank, the Bank of Japan, was concerned about the potential impact of an appreciating yen on Japan's export-oriented economy. In response to the Saudi decision, the Bank of Japan intervened in the currency market to strengthen the competitiveness of Japanese exports and keep the yen weak. This limited the yen's appeal as a reserve and trading currency.

Third, the United States responded to the Saudi decision by increasing its military presence in the Middle East and strengthening its relationship with Saudi Arabia. This reinforced the importance of the United States as a strategic partner to Saudi Arabia and limited the potential for the yen to replace the U.S. dollar in oil transactions.

After first announcing in 1989 that it would accept yen payments, Saudi Arabia eventually decided to return to using the U.S. dollar as the primary currency for oil payments.
This was due to the fact that the U.S. dollar remains the dominant currency in global trade and finance, and the yen has not been widely accepted as an international currency. Currently, the yen is not used for oil payments.

The Euro
When the euro was introduced in 1999, it was seen as a potential competitor to the U.S. dollar.
The euro quickly became the world's second most traded currency, and its share of global foreign exchange reserves has steadily increased.
In 2000, the euro's share of global foreign exchange reserves was about 18%, while the U.S. dollar's share was 71%.

By 2020, the euro's share had risen to about 20%, while the US dollar's share had fallen to about 60%.
The rise of the euro as a global currency has been driven by the growing importance of the European Union as a trading bloc and political force, as well as the euro's status as a stable currency.
However, there are several reasons why it has yet to replace the U.S. dollar as the reserve currency in the global financial system.

One of the biggest reasons is the comparative inferiority of the system and liquidity of the US financial markets.
The U.S. has the world's largest economy and most developed financial system, with extensive and liquid markets for stocks, bonds, and other financial instruments.

The stability and credibility of the U.S. financial system makes the U.S. dollar attractive.
The Eurozone, on the other hand, has a relatively small economy and less developed financial markets.

The European Central Bank (ECB) is a relatively new central bank, founded in 1998, and the euro has not yet achieved the same level of trust and confidence as the US dollar.

Another factor is the geopolitical and economic influence of the United States. The US is a global superpower with significant military and economic influence around the world, which gives the US dollar a unique position in international trade.

The Eurozone, on the other hand, is made up of several countries with different economic and political interests, making it difficult to establish a coherent and unified approach to financial policy.

Finally, there is the issue of the eurozone's sovereign debt crisis, which began in 2009 and exposed the weaknesses and vulnerabilities of the eurozone's financial system.

This has undermined confidence in the euro and made investors more cautious about holding large amounts of euros.

While the euro is an important currency in the global financial system, it has yet to match the dominance of the US dollar as a reserve currency.

The yuan

China has been working to increase the global use of the yuan in recent years.

In 2016, the yuan was included in the International Monetary Fund's (IMF) reserve currency basket, giving it legitimacy as an international currency.

China has also worked to promote the use of the yuan as a payment currency for oil. China is the world's largest importer of crude oil and has been increasing the use of the yuan in international trade to reduce its dependence on the U.S. dollar.

In 2018, China launched a yuan-denominated crude oil futures contract, the first futures contract priced in yuan and traded on a major international exchange.

And it is gradually expanding its reach by allowing Russia to use the yuan as a settlement currency for its crude oil.

China has also signed currency swap agreements with other countries, including Russia, Malaysia, and South Korea, allowing them to trade directly with China using the yuan instead of the dollar.

In 2021, it is estimated that 60% of the world's foreign exchange reserves are in dollars, compared to 2% in yuan.

To promote the use of its currency in international trade, China has provided many loans to middle-income and underdeveloped countries, including African countries.

This strategy is part of China's policy to promote the yuan as a global reserve currency and reduce its dependence on the U.S. dollar in international trade.
To take the lead in infrastructure projects and other development, China lends to other countries through several financial institutions, including the China Development Bank and the Export-Import Bank of China.

These loans are often denominated in yuan, and in doing so, it seeks to expand the international use of the currency.
While the euro, yen, and yuan have worked hard to become part of the oil settlement currencies that were instrumental in the U.S. gaining reserve currency status, the U.S. dollar still accounts for about 90% of global oil transactions.

However, in addition to the U.S. dollar, Russia uses the euro and Chinese yuan to pay for its oil exports, and Iran also uses non-dollar currencies such as the euro and Indian rupee to pay for its oil exports due to U.S. sanctions that limit its access to the U.S. financial system.

While these currencies threaten the U.S. position as a reserve currency, the U.S. dollar remains the dominant currency in the global economy.
In 2021, about 60% of the world's foreign exchange reserves are held in U.S. dollars, and about 40% of global trade is conducted in U.S. dollars.

The difference between speculation and investment

Speculation is the act of engaging in risky financial transactions for profit, and involves taking risks by buying or selling assets such as stocks, commodities, and real estate based on the belief that their value will increase or decrease in the future.

Speculation differs from investment in that speculation is based more on emotional factors, such as market conditions at the time, than on a rational judgment of value, and speculation is an extreme form of risk-taking that seeks to capitalize on opportunities and make large profits without the certainty of winning.

While both investing and speculating are related to the financial markets, they have different goals, strategies, and risk appetites.
Here are the main differences between the two concepts
1. Objective
In terms of objective, investing is about generating profits over a long period of time, while speculation aims to generate quick returns in a relatively short period of time.
For example, a person who participates in a diversified portfolio of stocks and bonds with the aim of generating stable returns over the long term can be said to be investing, while a person who buys speculative stocks with the hope of making a quick profit in a few days or weeks can be said to be speculating.

2. Risk
Investing tends to involve a lower level of risk than speculation because it typically involves a more diversified portfolio of assets.

According to the theory of portfolio diversification, investors try to lower their risk by putting all their eggs in one basket of low-correlation investments, while those with speculative objectives are looking to make high returns in a short period of time, so they try to stick to one particular investment.

For example, someone who invests in an index fund, which is based on an index of the entire stock market, may experience lower volatility and risk than someone who invests in a single high-risk stock, but speculation is likely to involve a higher level of risk because someone with a speculative disposition is betting on a single stock or asset to make a quick profit.

3. Holding period vs. investment period

Investing is generally more likely to involve holding assets for a longer period of time than speculation, so investing is more likely to involve holding assets for a longer period of time and speculation is more likely to involve holding assets for a shorter period of time.

For example, a person who contributes a certain amount of money to a pension savings account from a young age to save for retirement can be considered to be investing, while a person who buys stocks with the intention of making a profit in a few weeks or months can be considered to be engaging in speculative activities.

4. Information and analysis

Investing often involves a more thorough analysis of assets and markets, while speculation tends to rely more on rumors and intuition.

People who invest in mutual funds or exchange-traded index funds typically do research on the fund's holdings, performance, and fees, and consider future changes in the economic environment before investing. However, someone who speculates on a single stock may not do a thorough analysis of the stock's fundamentals and may buy a stock based on rumors from friends or intuition.

In conclusion, investing and speculating are both about putting money into financial assets with the goal of making a profit, but they differ in their purpose, level of risk, holding and investment periods, and the amount of analysis and review involved.

History of speculation before the 17th century

While the phenomenon of financial speculation as we understand it today was not fully developed until the advent of modern capital markets, there are examples of speculation in human history prior to the 17th century.

The earliest historical record of financial speculation dates back to the 2nd century B.C. Roman speculation on the Publicani, the government agencies responsible for collecting taxes and building temples.

At the time, the Romans were obsessed with profit, and the side effects of speculation left many commoners impoverished and mentally distressed.

In the 3rd century BC, the first currency crisis in history occurred in Thrace.

After the introduction of the credit system, the speculative demand for good quality currency increased, causing prices to skyrocket, leaving the entire city without access to basic necessities and supplies.

Examples of speculation also occurred during the Tang Dynasty (618-907) in China, when the government issued paper money backed by silver coins.

As the notes became widely accepted, their value began to fluctuate with the price of silver, leading to speculation and price swings. At one point, the value of paper money plummeted, causing panic and economic chaos.

In medieval Europe, merchants would make a profit by purchasing goods at their place of origin and then selling them in places where they expected prices to be higher. This type of trading was known as "arbitrage" and was seen in commodities such as grains, spices, and textiles.

Financial speculation as we understand it today did not fully emerge until the development of modern capital markets in the 17th century, but there are many examples of such speculation throughout human history.

Copyright © 2023 by Anddy Park

All rights reserved

No part of this book may be reproduced or transmitted in any form or by any means, electronic or mechanical, including photocopying, recording, or by any information storage and retrieval system, without permission in writing from the author.

For more information, email : anddy.park2014@gmail.com

www.ingramcontent.com/pod-product-compliance
Lightning Source LLC
Chambersburg PA
CBHW081431220526
45466CB00008B/2338

9 798393 871505